INNSBRUCK
HALL IN TIROL

Photo Credits: Photos on front and back covers by Günther Haas/Innsbruck. Aigner: p. 81; Archiv Alpenzoo: p. 61; Alpine Luftbild: p. 4; Bacher-Bliem: p. 82; Grassmayr: p. 56; Haas: p. 7, 10 (top), 11, 12, 14, 15, 16 (left and right), 17 (left and right), 19, 20, 23, 24 (top), 30, 31 (top and bottom), 32, 33, 36, 37 (top and bottom), 38 (top and bottom), 39, 40, 41 (left and right), 42 (top), 43, 44, 45, 46, 47, 48/49, 52, 54, 55, 57, 62, 63, 68, 71, 73, 76 (top and bottom), 84, 85, 90 (top and bottom), 93, 95; Hofburg/Schlossverwaltung: p. 10 (bottom), 24 (bottom left and right); Holy: p. 58; Dr. Hye: p. 9; Oberarzbacher: p. 18; Tiroler Landeskundliches Museum - Zeughaus: p. 50, 89; Tiroler Landesmuseum Ferdinandeum: p. 25, 42 (bottom), 59 (top); Tiroler Volkskunstmuseum: p. 26 (top and bottom), 27, 59 (bottom), 60 (top); Tourismusverband Hall in Tirol: p. 87; Dr. Wagner: p. 16 (bottom), 22.

Text: Mag. Monika Niederwolfsgruber, Innsbruck
Translation from the German: Mary Heaney Margreiter
Editor-in-Chief: Reinhard Strohmeier, KOMPASS Rum/Innsbruck

We would like to express our gratitude to Dr. Franz-Heinz Hye, Director of the Innsbruck Municipal Archive, for reviewing the chapter "Chronicle of Innsbruck" and to the museums for providing slides.

Information in a city guide changes almost constantly in these fast-paced times, and the editors thus accept no liability for the guide despite having made every effort to ensure its reliability. As experience continuously shows, errors are never entirely avoidable. The editors are grateful for any corrections and suggestions you care to make. Please send these to the following address:

Fleischmann & Mair GmbH, Kaplanstraße 2, A-6063 Rum/Innsbruck, Austria
or to
Heinz Fleischmann GmbH & Co., Nymphenburger Straße 47, D-80335 Munich, Germany
or to
KOMPASS – Fleischmann Srl, Loc. Ghiaie 166/D, I-38014 Gardolo/TN.

First edition 1996
Publisher's No. 502
ISBN 3-87051-339-x

CONTENTS

PREFACE 5

A PROFILE OF THE ALPINE CITY
- Geography – Geology – Climate 6
- Chronicle of Innsbruck 8

INNSBRUCK'S ATTRACTIONS
- Innsbruck's Attractions from A to Z 13
- Tour of the City 46
- On the Trail of the Famous 50
- Museums 55
- Especially for Kids 61

FAVORITE EXCURSIONS IN AND AROUND INNSBRUCK 63

IMPORTANT INFORMATION – TIPS
- Information 69
- Accommodations 70
- For Emergencies 70
- Sightseeing (Walks and Drives) 71
- Traffic (Car, Train, Plane, Public Transportation, Cable Cars) 72
- Culture – Entertainment – Relaxation – Tyrolean Craftsmen 76
- Sports 83
- Post Office and Telephone Service 86
- Consulates and Embassies 86

HALL IN TIROL
- Chronicle of Hall in Tirol 88
- City Sights 90
- Museums 94
- Information 95

INDEX 96

Welcome to the Capital of Tyrol! Welcome to Innsbruck!

Whether you've only come for a short holiday or you live here permanently, you'll want to get better acquainted with the capital of Tyrol. Our "Guide to Innsbruck" invites you to take interesting walks through town, exciting mountain hikes on well-tended trails through magnificent forests, while familiarizing you with the most interesting and beautiful aspects of the "City in the Mountains" and its neighbor Hall in Tirol, the old salt and coinage city and jewel of the Middle Ages. This guide will provide you with all the background information you need for your stay in Tyrol.

A relaxing stroll through Innsbruck naturally calls for time and interest, and you'll want to stop and take a break in a quiet place like the Court Palace, Rapoldi Park or one of the peaceful, hidden courtyards in the Old City. Whether you just want to read up on the sights or need specific information, the KOMPASS Guide to Innsbruck is the place to look, with all points easy to locate in the Index.

The guide starts by introducing you to the geography and the colorful history of "Inspruk." This is followed by a brief look at the city's cultural offerings. You'll also learn what will interest sports fans and where to find children's entertainment in Innsbruck.

But many visitors to Innsbruck are looking for something more adventuresome. Try the short and long hikes around Innsbruck or some of the other exciting ideas on how to spend your holiday time. Next comes an introduction to some of Innsbruck's more famous sons and daughters. Depending on your personal taste, maybe we can help you choose a delicious meal in one of the Old City's many tempting restaurants offering authentic "Tyrolean specialties."

The next point on your itinerary is a "tour" of the city, with maps of the city and its surroundings getting you around town quickly and easily. The list of "Attractions from A to Z" and of museums is handy for anyone short of time. To fill in any gaps, this handy guide includes an extensive reference section with in-depth information and tips on accommodations, traffic connections, post office and telephone services, consulates and embassies etc.

Now all you have to do is take the KOMPASS Guide to Innsbruck in hand and discover the city for yourself.

KOMPASS

◂ *Innsbruck's Old City*

Innsbruck: A Profile of the Alpine City

GEOGRAPHY – GEOLOGY – CLIMATE

Approximately 128,000 people live in Innsbruck, the capital of Tyrol. The inner city lies at 575 m (1,886 ft) above sea level. The city area of approximately 105 km^2 is surrounded by mountains. To the north the city is enclosed by the imposing Nordkette and the Gleirsch-Kette still further north, with the highest peaks being the Western Praxmarerkarspitze (2,638 m) and the Patscherkofel (2,247 m) to the south. Of this total area, approximately 31% is Alpine wasteland, 36% woodlands, 23% arable land and the remaining 10% is inhabitable. The city spans 18 km from north to south and 11 km from east to west. The Innsbruck city limits comprise the following districts (year of incorporation in parentheses): Inner City and Wilten (1904), Pradl (1904), Hötting (1938), Mühlau (1938), Arzl (1940), Amras (1938), Igls (1942) and Vill (1942).

The Inn Valley with its east-west orientation stretches from Landeck, over Innsbruck to Kufstein. At Innsbruck the Wipp Valley branches off southwards, climbing to Brenner Pass, the border to Italy's South Tyrol. Just a few kilometers west of Innsbruck, the road over Zirler Berg takes you to Scharnitz and Bavaria. This location at a geographic crossroads has been vital to the city's development through the ages. Consequently, the Inn Valley and the terraces on both sides of it were settled in very early times.

Innsbruck's topographical setting is characterized by three different rock formations. To the south are the so-called "Slate Alps" (Schieferalpen), covered with dense forests and exemplified by the Tuxer Alpine Foothills and the Patscherkofel. There are also the formations of the Brenner Mesozoic, found at the Kalkkögel and the Serles, typically with limestone caps resting on a crystalline basement. Finally, there are the massive limestones of the Nordkette. Fissures throughout the Nordkette limestones are the major source of Innsbruck's excellent drinking water.

Innsbruck's broad southern exposure (to the Wipp Valley) is an open invitation to one of the city's most distinctive climatic features: the foehn. This warm southern wind blowing strongly at high altitudes produces a conspicuous rise in temperature on the valley floor and good visibility for miles around. The foehn occurs more frequently in the spring and autumn. The warm, gusting winds raise the average monthly temperature in relation to other comparable locations. The average summer temperatures measure 18° C with record highs at 36° C. The

Foehn in the Inn Valley

lowest temperature was recorded at –27° C in February 1957. Innsbruck first started keeping precipitation records in 1781. Long-range statistics show that February, March, October and November have the least precipitation. As far as the number of hours of sunshine, September is the most pleasant month in Innsbruck. Winter sports enthusiasts are primarily interested in snow conditions, and these can vary strongly from year to year. However, you can find snow anytime of year in one of the many ski areas around Innsbruck. As an alternative, there are always the year-round ski resorts in the Stubai Valley, Oetz Valley and in Hintertux.

From this brief description you can glean some of the many features of the "City in the Mountains." It's no wonder countless guests flock to Innsbruck throughout the year to take in the richness of her culture and history as well as the awe-inspiring mountain scenery. Moreover, Innsbruck is an important host city for trade fairs and congresses, a favorite place for shopping, an internationally recognized university city with approx. 27,000 students from around the world and since 1964 also a bishop's seat. Innsbruck became world famous as host of the Winter Olympic Games in 1964 and 1976. Both Olympic villages with their many high-rises in the eastern part of the city and several sports facilities are reminiscent of those days. We recommend you take in the view of the entire city from Hungerburg in the north or Bergisel in the south.

Prehistoric Era
The Illyrians and the Rhaetians settle the terraces around the Innsbruck basin, which were well sheltered from flooding. **Urnfields** have been discovered in Wilten, Hötting and Mühlau. Turmbühel near Vill is the site of finds dating back to the La Tène culture.

15 BC
The Roman Empire rapidly expands under **Drusus** and **Tiberius** and extends as far as the Alps. It is here that the **Roman province of Rhaetia,** which also includes Innsbruck, is founded.

46 AD
The **Via Claudia Augusta** is constructed, a road beginning in Italy and winding over Reschen Pass and Fern Pass or Brenner Pass, Seefeld and Garmisch, ultimately ending in Augsburg.

2nd – 5th century AD
The **Romans** erect Veldidena (in present-day Wilten) as an **outpost** in order to protect the Brenner Road. It is then expanded to a fortress.

6th century AD
The **Baiuvarii** invade from the north and settle in the Inn Valley. Tyrol thus becomes part of the Bavarian duchy.

1027
The German emperors take the strategically important mountain lands, also described as "Territory in the Mountains," away from the Bavarian dukes and grant possession of it to the **bishops of Brixen and Trent.** The bishops of Brixen, in turn, hand over Tyrol's individual valleys to different aristocratic houses as feudal tenure.

1138
The **Premonstratensian Abbey** in Wilten, erected by Bishop Reginbert of Brixen, receives papal recognition.

1165/1170
Bishop Otto of Brixen grants the countship in the mid-Inn Valley between Melach and Ziller as well as the countship in the Eisack Valley to the Counts of Andechs. Already in power and in possession of Ambras Castle, ca. 1165/1170 the **Counts of Andechs** establish the market town of "Inspruk" on the left bank of the Inn. At this time, they construct the "Innbrücke" or Inn Bridge, hence the city's name. They become the most influential rulers in the Inn Valley, and Innsbruck becomes the focal point of their lands. When their market on the left bank of the Inn (present-day St. Nikolaus) grows too small for them, they trade with Wilten Abbey in 1180 for the land on the right bank of the Inn, the site of today's Old City.

c. 1167/1183
The name **"Inspruk"** is first mentioned in official records.

c. 1187/1204
Innsbruck rises to the status of a **city** with a city wall and trenches.

The charter then acquired by the city is in

1239
renewed and confirmed by **Duke Otto of Andechs.** The Andechs' castle and residence were located near the former Inn Barracks or Viktor Dankl Barracks at the Inn Bridge across from the Ottoburg (see Herzog-Otto-Strasse).

1248
The **Counts of Andechs die out** and are succeeded by the Counts of Tyrol, who are then succeeded by the Counts of Tyrol-Gorizia in 1253.

1281
Count Meinhard II of Tyrol-Gorizia, the "Founder of Tyrol" (see Meinhardstrasse), acquires from Wilten Abbey Innsbruck's "new city" or today's Maria-Theresien-Strasse.

Small city seal with the oldest horizontal depiction of the Inn Bridge (1325)

1363
The Dukes of Austria obtain Tyrol and consequently Innsbruck through **Countess Margaret Maultasch,** granddaughter of Meinhard II.

1420
Duke Frederick IV, "with the Empty Purse," (see Herzog-Friedrich-Strasse) transfers his residence from Castle Tyrol in Meran to the New Court (see Goldenes Dachl) in Innsbruck.

1446
Duke Sigismund, "the Rich" (see Herzog-Sigmund-Ufer), only son of Duke Frederick, becomes **sole ruler.** It is during his reign that in 1460 the present-day Court Palace is built.

1477
Duke Sigismund transfers the **mint** from Meran to **Hall in Tirol.**

1490
Duke Sigismund steps down in favor of his cousin's son, later **Emperor Maximilian I** (see Maximilianstrasse). During the reign of Maximilian, Innsbruck becomes an important cultural center. He is responsible for construction of the "Zeughaus" or armory (see Museums, Tiroler Landeskundliches Museum – Zeughaus) and the Little Golden Roof (see Goldenes Dachl); the Court Church (see Hofkirche) memorializes his name. He, his court and Innsbruck's status benefit from the wealth reaped from the silver mines in Schwaz and the salt mines in Hall.

1473 – 1550
The **Türing family, stonemasons and architects** from Memmingen in Germany, work for three consecutive generations as court and municipal architects, significantly influencing the look of the city.

1564
The ruler of Tyrol, **Archduke Ferdinand II,** remodels Ambras Castle in the Renaissance style (see Schloss Ambras).

Don't miss the display of armor in Ambras Castle

1602
Archduke Maximilian the "Deutschmeister," brother of Emperor Rudolf II, becomes the ruler of Tyrol.

1618 – 1648
The Thirty Years' War barely affects Tyrol; Innsbruck itself is spared. The Tyrolean sovereign at this time is **Leopold V,** who is married to Claudia de Medici (see Jesuitenkirche).

1665
On the death of Archduke Sigismund Francis the Tyrolean line of the House of Habsburg dies out and **Emperor Leopold I** incorporates Tyrol and other possessions with all the other Habsburg lands. Tyrol thus feels the increasing influence of Vienna. Up to 1918, the Austrian monarch is also the sovereign of Tyrol.

1669
Emperor Leopold I founds the **University of Innsbruck** on Herrengasse.

17th/18th Century
The **Gumpp family of master builders** are foremost in planning and construction in Innsbruck.

1765
Empress Maria Theresa visits Innsbruck. She orders the renovation of the Court Palace (see Hofburg).

Oil painting "Maria Theresa" in Innsbruck's Court Palace

1805
As a result of the **Treaty of Bratislava,** Tyrol falls to Bavaria, a close ally of Napoleon.

1809
Andreas Hofer successfully leads the **Battles of Bergisel** (see Bergisel and Andreas-Hofer-Strasse). He takes over the government of Tyrol. However, in the same year, Tyrol is once again invaded by **Bavarian troops** and remains under Bavarian rule until

1814
when Tyrol is returned to **Austria** at the **Congress of Vienna.**

19th Century
The **Industrial Age** sees **construction of the railroad** across Brenner Pass, through the Inn Valley, tunnelling under the Arlberg and to Mittenwald. Innsbruck thus develops to a major European transportation junction for east-west and north-south rail traffic. Population subsequently booms, and in 1904 the city limits are expanded by annexing the first new district.

World War I
The **Treaty of St. Germain** is signed in 1919 and moves Austria's southern border back to Brenner Pass; South Tyrol is awarded to Italy.

World War II
Innsbruck serves as the **capital of the Nazi province** of Tyrol and Vorarlberg. The city suffers severe damage due to heavy **bombing** from 1943 to 1945.

1945 – 1955
Innsbruck is **occupied by the French army.**

1955
Austria regains full sovereignty through the **Vienna Treaty.**

1964
Innsbruck becomes a **bishopric city.** Until the end of World War I and from 1925 to 1964, it had been under the apostolic administration of the Diocese of Brixen (see Dom).

1964 and 1976
Innsbruck hosts the **Winter Olympic Games.**

These many centuries of colorful history have left their mark on Innsbruck and Tyrol, bequeathing the city a wealth of sights, cultural monuments and, above all, an impressive Old City.

The Inn Promenade in Innsbruck's Mariahilf

Innsbruck's Attractions

Be sure not to miss these Sights!

- ★ The **Golden Roof (Goldenes Dachl)** is Innsbruck's most photographed sight.
- ★ The **"Black Statues" ("Schwarze Mannder")** surround the empty tomb of Emperor Maximilian I in the Court Church (Hofkirche).
- ★ The recently – and magnificently – renovated **Cathedral** of Innsbruck was built in the early 18th century and contains a modern crypt.
- ★ The buildings in the **Old City** date back to the 15th and 16th centuries.
- ★ You can climb the **City Tower** and enjoy the view of the Old City and the very unique mountain panorama.
- ★ The **Museum of Tyrolean Folk Art (Tiroler Volkskunstmuseum)** displays nativity crèches, examples of traditional dress, models of houses and farmhouses, carnival masks and costumes, among other Tyrolean artefacts.
- ★ The Grassmayr **Bell Museum (Glockenmuseum)** memorably illustrates the fine craft of bell-casting.
- ★ The splendid **Ambras Castle (Schloss Ambras)** was built in the Renaissance period and houses, among other treasures, a collection of armor.
- ★ The **Olympic Ski Jump (Olympia-Sprungschanze)** is impressive in itself while offering a terrific vista of the city, towered over by the imposing Nordkette mountains.
- ★ The **Alpine Zoo (Alpenzoo),** whose renown extends well beyond Innsbruck and Tyrol, is a delight for young and old alike.

INNSBRUCK'S ATTRACTIONS FROM A TO Z

★ Altes Rathaus – Stadtturm (Old City Hall – City Tower)

The **Old City Hall** was built in 1358. Georg Türing renovated it in 1543. In 1691, after a fire and an earthquake, it was rebuilt by Johann Martin Gumpp the Elder. The mayor of Innsbruck had his office here until 1897 and again in the 1990s.

The unique, 56-meter-tall City Hall Tower, also known as the **City Tower,** was constructed around 1450 and served into the 19th century as, among other things, a fire watch tower. In 1560, the pointed roofs were replaced with dome-shaped roofs. On the southern wall, there is a 16th century sundial fresco. A gallery encircles the tower 33 meters above the ground, giving a marvellous view of the Old City below and of the mountain panorama surrounding Innsbruck. The fire alarm bell was cast in 1468; the bell that strikes the hour, decorated with the coats of arms of both the city and of the

◂ ***The Golden Roof, Innsbruck's best known building***

The 15th-century City Tower

bell's donor, dates back to 1560; and the small bell decorated with the Madonna and crucifix and labelled "Grassmayr/Wilten" was made in 1740.
City Tower: Herzog-Friedrich-Strasse 21. Telephone: 57 59 62.
Open daily from

May 1 – June 30	10 am – 5 pm
July 1 – Aug 31	10 am – 6 pm
Sept 1 – Oct 31	10 am – 5 pm

Annasäule (St. Anne's Column)

As an expression of gratitude for delivering Tyrol from Bavarian invasion on St. Anne's Day (July 26th) in 1703, the Tyrolean legislature erected this monument in the middle of Maria-Theresien-Strasse. A statue of the Virgin Mary upon a crescent moon thrones atop the Corinthian column of red marble. The pedestal is surrounded by statues of St. Cassian, St. Vigilius, St. George and St. Anne, made by the sculptor Christoph Benedettti of Trent.

Basilika und Pfarrkirche Mariae Empfängnis (Basilica and Parish Church of the Immaculate Conception in Wilten)

Legend has it that Roman legionaries once worshiped before a picture of the Virgin Mary beneath four trees on this very spot. The church was first documented in 870. In the early 14th and 15th centuries it was expanded, and in the early 18th century it was renovated in the Baroque style. Between 1751 and 1755, the Tyrolean priest Franz de Paula Penz was charged with supervising its reconstruction; it ranks along with the parish church in Gossensass, South Tyrol, as his most important work. The new building was designed by the sculptor Josef Stapf of Füssen. The result is the most impressive Rococo religious building in North Tyrol. A large, open square in front of the church allows the visitor to appreciate it all the more. Construction of the crypt in the 18th century brought Roman masonry to light. In 1957, Pope Pius XII elevated the church to the status of basilica. The church consists of a single nave with a two-tower façade. A 19th-century mosaic of Our Lady of the Four Columns graces the eastern outer wall. The doors decorated with vine carvings are also admirable. The church's interior is embellished with white and gold stuccowork by Franz Xavier Feichtmayr and Anton Gigl and with murals and ceiling frescoes by Matthäus Günther of Augsburg. These artists are among the most highly regarded of their age. All the ceiling fres-

Wilten Cemetery with the Basilica and Nordkette mountains

coes depict the Virgin Mary and her Old Testament predecessors: in the choir, the Virgin Mary as an intercessor in the company of angels; in the eastern dome, Esther; in the central dome, Christ with the Cross and the Virgin Mary; in the western dome, Judith. The murals at the side chapels depict the saints to whom the particular altar is dedicated: St. Joseph, St. Catherine, St. Theresa together with St. John of the Cross, and the Apostle Andreas. The high altar with its four columns of Untersberg marble (probably remnants of an earlier building) is certainly worth seeing. The columns support an enormous baldachin, beneath which gleams the miracle-working statue of Madonna with child. Ninety centimeters tall and made of sandstone, the statue dates back to the 14th century. This so-called "Our Lady of the Four Columns" has been venerated by pilgrims for many centuries. Beneath the statue glisten two Baroque candelabra in the shape of angels; they are attributed to Andreas Faistenberger. Georg Grassmayr and Michelangelo Unterberger painted the pictures for the side altars in 1729 and 1756, respectively. The side altars themselves were built by Josef Stapf, who, together with Franz Xavier Nissl, also created the marble statues at these altars. The only votive picture remaining in the church hangs on the southern pilaster; the others are kept in the nearby Wilten Abbey Church. Painted in 1418, it depicts Duke Frederick the Penniless together with his friend Mülinen. The former commissioned the picture as a sign of gratitude upon regaining power.

The neighborhood of Wilten with the snow-covered Nordkette mountains

The papal coat of arms above the main entrance showing that the church was elevated to the status of basilica

Rococo splendor of the Basilica's interior

Bergisel

This 748-meter-tall wooded hill is located in the south of the city at the end of the Wipp Valley. In 1809, it was the site of the famous Bergisel battles. It was here that, led by Andreas Hofer, the Tyrolean peasants defended their homeland against French and Bavarian invaders. From 1816 on, the Tyrolean Rifle (Kaiserjäger) Regiment used this plateau as a shooting range. The Regiment received this area as a gift from the Wilten Abbey Church for the purpose of building the shooting range and a memorial. The enormous **bronze monument** of the **freedom fighter Andreas Hofer** stands in the park; a parking lot and café are nearby. The monument was cast by Heinrich Natter from metal melted down from French cannons seized in combat. In 1894, it was unveiled in the presence of Emperor

The Andreas Hofer Monument at Bergisel

The Tyrolean flag flies at the Bergisel Museum

Franz Josef I. In 1962, having been blown up by Italian neo-fascists, it had to be restored. On the 20th of February of each year, the day on which Tyrol's heroic freedom fighter Andreas Hofer met his death, a wreath is laid at the foot of the statue and a small ceremony held. In the nearby chapel, you can visit the grave of the founder of the Tyrolean Rifle Regiment, Field Marshal Franz Philipp Fenner von Fennberg. The Bergisel Museum / Tyrolean Rifle (Kaiserjäger) Regiment Museum adjoins the chapel (see Museums).

Büchsenhausen

In 1539, the metal caster and master gunsmith, Georg Löffler, built this residence at Weiherburggasse 5 – 13. The main building served as his house, and one of the neighboring buildings as his workshop. It was here that

Büchsenhausen in St. Nikolaus

he cast two bells and a figure for the mausoleum of Emperor Maximilian in Innsbruck's Court Church. The residence changed hands several times over the years. In the 17th century, its renovation was most likely overseen by Johann Martin Gumpp the Elder. In more recent years, the building has again undergone major renovation. On house No. 7, the sundial painted in the early 18th century is of special note. On the third floor of house No. 9, there is a chapel dedicated to St. John of Nepomuk, built in 1698. In the nave, a Baroque intersecting vault, an early 18th century wrought-iron choir grille and a carved Baroque altar with a reliquary deserve special attention.

★ Dom und Propsteipfarrkirche zum hl. Jakobus (St. James' Cathedral and Provostry Church)

The Cathedral of Innsbruck reigns over Cathedral Square (Domplatz). The eastern side of this church building – the first of the High Baroque period in Tyrol – adjoins the Court Palace (Hofburg). The dome and both towers can be seen from very far away.

The church was first documented in 1180. It was renovated and expanded between the 14th and the 16th centuries and destroyed by an earthquake in 1689. It was rebuilt between 1717 and 1724 according to the plans of the master builder Johann Jakob Herkommer of Füssen, modeled after the Church of St. Mang in Füssen. The brothers Egid and Cosmas Damian Asam of Munich created the ceiling frescoes and stuccowork in 1722. The interior furnishings are from the period 1725 to 1732. The church was badly damaged by bombing in 1944 and was rebuilt and expanded in the post-war years, from 1946 to 1950. The exterior restoration took place in 1973; the interior restoration, including reconstruction of the crypt, was accomplished between 1991 and 1993. Until 1643, the church was affiliated with Wilten Abbey. Thereafter, it was an independent parish church and, from 1904 on, a provostry church. It was elevated to the status of cathedral in 1964, when Innsbruck parted from the Diocese of Brixen, South Tyrol, and became an independent diocese. The two towers dominate the Cathedral's external appearance. Since 1982, the left-hand tower has housed the 47 bells of the Innsbruck Peace Chimes (Innsbrucker Friedensglockenspiel). The severe façade of the church nave, made of gray nagelfluh stone, is enlivened by the light marble borders. In the niches, the following limestone statues can be found: the patron saints of Brixen (Cassian, Ingenuin and Alvin), the Tyrolean saints Romedius and Notburga as well as the saints Hartmann, Heinrich of Bozen and Mary Magdalene. The Virgin Mary is at the center. Above, in the gable, is an equestrian statue of St. James. The statues were made by Hans Andre between 1938 and 1960. Since the last renovation, the interior glows with new splendor. The pillars dividing the nave are of red marble and the capitals are partly gilded. Through the tall, central dome, light flows over the high

The Cathedral of Innsbruck rises form a sea of roofs

altar and floods the church. The high altar, built between 1726 and 1729, was a gift of the prince-bishop of Brixen, Kaspar Ignaz Count Künigl. The famous, miracle-working "Our Lady of Perpetual Help" by Lucas Cranach the Elder is especially notable. Painted around 1520, it has adorned the altar since 1650. It is the best known Madonna in the entire German-speaking Alpine region. A magnificent silver antependium decorates the high altar year-round, with the exception of Lent and Advent, and was a gift of Karl Philipp of The Palatinate in 1712. On the southern wall of the choir hangs a modern tapestry made by Elfi Baumgartner in 1974. The ceiling frescoes, the work of Cosmas Damian Asam, illustrate scenes from the life of St. James the Apostle: in the choir, he leads the Christians against the Saracens in Spain; in the transept, he admonishes people to worship the Virgin Mary; in the nave, he intercedes on behalf of the poor and protects Innsbruck, Tyrol, Austria and the entire Catholic Church. Egid Asam, the brother of the above-mentioned artist, created the stuccowork in the Early Rococo style. There are further works of interest in the nave: marble altars from 1731; the reliquary shrines from the Rococo period; the pulpit, made by Nikolaus Moll in 1725, decorated with the coat of arms of its donor, Zech-Fieger. A precious Baroque wrought-iron grille separates the choir from the nave.

◂ ***The high altar with the Madonna shines with new splendour***

The organ was built between 1723 and 1725. The paintings at the side altars, Assumption of the Virgin Mary, St. Sebastian and St. John of Nepomuk, were painted by Johann Georg Grassmayr. A wooden crucifix from the 16th century at another side altar was carved with great artistry.

In the left-hand transept is the tomb of Archduke Maximilian, a Grand Master of the Teutonic Order, who died in 1618. This tomb was a joint effort: designed by Caspar Grass and cast by Heinrich Reinhart, it was erected in 1629. The four spiral columns supporting the structure are adorned with animal figures. In 1954, Archduke Eugene was also buried here.

Domplatz (Cathedral Square)

House No. 2 on Domplatz (known until 1964 as the Parish Square, or Pfarrplatz) originally belonged to the cathedral chapter of Brixen and was called Brixen House (Brixner Haus). In 1633, its ownership was transferred to Stams Monastery and ever since it has been called Stams House (Stamser Haus). House No. 5 served in the 16th century as "The Singing School of the City Parish" ("Stadtpfarr Singschule"). It is now the residence of the bishop of Innsbruck. A Baroque stone portal decorates the entry. House No. 6, once the rectory, is now the provostry headquarters. The stone portal dates back to the 17th century.

★ Goldenes Dachl (Golden Roof)

This building was constructed under the auspices of Duke Frederick IV in the early 15th century.

Reliefs and frescoes on the Golden Roof

In former times it was also called the New Court (Neuhof). Between 1494 and 1496, Niclas Türing the Elder, in the service of Emperor Maximilian I, redesigned the original oriel as a spectator's box with Gothic vaults. From here, members of the court could watch the jousting tournaments and performances on the square below. The two-storied oriel is 16 meters wide. The roof itself is 3.7 meters tall and bears 2,600 gilded copper shingles, hence the building's name. Beneath the roof's edge there is a frieze of many different animals. Numerous reliefs by Niclas Türing the Elder on the front of the loggia depict Emperor Maximilian I with his wives Maria Bianca Sforza and Marie of Burgundy. They also portray acrobatic dancers. The carved reliefs on the bottom row are also the work of Gregor Türing and represent the coats of arms of Austria, Hungary, the Austro-Hungarian Empire's Double Eagle, the King's Eagle, the coats of arms of Burgundy and Milan, and on the sides of the loggias, those of Styria and Tyrol. Jörg Kölderer's murals portray two banner-bearers with the flags of the Empire and of Tyrol. The original reliefs are on display in the Tyrolean State Museum Ferdinandeum.

The building has housed the **Olympic Museum (Olympia-Museum;** see Museums) since 1983. It also contains the Register Office and private apartments.

Heiligwasser – Wallfahrtskirche zur hl. Ottilie (Heiligwasser – Pilgrimage Church of St. Ottilia)

The name of this place (in English: Holy Water) derives from a nearby spring. Built in 1662, this pilgrimage church is located on a slope south of Igls at 1,240m above sea level. In 1945, Hans Andre painted the ceiling to show the Blessed Trinity, Christ Being Taken Down off the Cross, the Annunciation and the Birth of Mary. A Gothic Madonna with child graces the Baroque high altar. The church's interior and exterior have been thoroughly renovated in recent years.

The pilgrimage church at Heiligwasser is a popular retreat

Hofburg (Court Palace)

The original, late medieval fortress was built under Duke Sigismund the Rich around 1460 and served as the residence for Tyrol's sovereigns. Under Emperor Maximilian I, the building was renovated and enlarged around 1500 in the Late Gothic style and splendidly furnished. After a fire in the mid 16th century, Emperor Ferdinand I had an Italian architect remodel both interior and exterior in the Renaissance style. In 1754, Maria Theresa entrusted Johann Martin Gumpp the Younger with the complete remodeling of the palace, which he finished in 1770. Since then, the four-winged structure with its spacious courtyard embodies the radiant Late Baroque and Rococo styles. Innsbruck's Court Palace contains about 400 rooms. The state rooms, show rooms and reception rooms can be visited. The **Guard Room (Gardesaal)** contains a Rococo stove and portraits of important members of the Habsburg lineage, including Karl V of Lorraine, Maximilian I, Frederick IV the Penniless. The **Giants' Room (Riesensaal)** is so named because, according to legend, it was decorated in Maximilian's day with portraits of giants. There is much worth admiring in this room: the sumptuous Late Rococo decorations, the three-toned marble floor, the portraits of Maria Theresa and Franz I with their 16 children (painted in 1776), the three-part ceiling fresco by Franz Anton Maulpertsch depicting the triumph of the House of Habsburg-Lorraine. The **Lorraine Room (Lothringer Zimmer),** or Sovereign's Room (Fürstenzimmer), is furnished in the Rococo style and has a white marble fireplace. It is decorated with portraits of relatives of Emperor Francis I as well as of himself and Maria Theresa in Hungarian coronation regalia. The **Chapter Room (Kapitelzimmer)** is also furnished in the Rococo style and contains a magnificent stove and historical paintings from the period of Maria Theresa. **The Andreas Hofer Room (Andreas-Hofer-Zimmer)** is named after the hero of the Tyrolean battles for freedom. As Commander-in-Chief of Tyrol, he resided in the Court Palace from August to October 1809. The **Emperor's private**

The courtyard of the Court Palace with the dome of the Cathedral

The Tower Room

The Giants' Room

rooms (Kaiserappartements) consist of the Yellow Room (Gelbes Zimmer), the Pink Salon (Rosa Salon) and the Chinese Room (Chinesenzimmer). All three rooms are marvelously furnished in the Rococo style replete with stuccowork, chandeliers, allegorical tapestries and portraits. The **Palace Chapel (Hauskapelle)** is also on the south wing's second floor. In 1766, Maria Theresa had Nikolaus Pacassi convert the room where Emperor Franz I died (in 1765) into a chapel. This chapel is notable for its Rococo stuccowork, the painted relief above the altar, the oil painting of the Visitation of Mary and the Blessed Virgin at the Temple, the organ and other mementos of Maria Theresa.

Hofgarten (Court Garden)

Originating in the early 15th century out of the kitchen garden of Duke Leopold IV and Duke Frederick IV, the Court Garden was expanded in the 15th and 16th centuries. The beautifully tended **park grounds** have been open to the public since the early 19th century. The park is enclosed by a wall with wrought-iron gates dating back to the mid 19th century. Built around 1830, the **Music Pavilion** stands approximately in the center of the park. Today, concerts are often held within or in front of the pavilion. North of it is an open-air chessboard which attracts players and onlookers alike. **Fountains** have been placed to the north and south of the pavilion. Many benches, a playground and the Hofgartencafé invite the stroller to relax and rest. The **Monument to Archduke Eugene** was designed by the architect Clemens Holzmeister and erected in 1957. (Field Marshal Archduke Eugene was the last member of the House of Habsburg-Lorraine to reside in Innsbruck.) In the **Art Pavilion (Kunstpavillon),** once the Court Tea House, artists display their work in temporary exhibitions.

Hofkirche – Silberne Kapelle – "Neues Stift" (Court Church – Silver Chapel – "New Monastery")

Built between 1553 and 1563, this triple-nave church immediately adjoins the Franciscan Monastery on the one side and the Court Palace on the other. It was designed by the architect Andreas Crivelli of Trent, and Niclas Türing the Younger was entrusted with its construction. Emperor Ferdinand I commissioned the **mausoleum of Emperor Maximilian I,** his deceased grandfather, and was responsible for its construction. As early as the age of 40, Emperor Maximilian planned a monumental mausoleum for himself, without, however, specifying where it was to be erected. Forty larger-than-life bronze figures (members of his family and ancestors, saints related to the Habsburgs and busts of ancient Roman emperors) were to pay him their last respects. He conducted extensive research to determine the appearance, dress and coat of arms of each personage. Maximilian commissioned the most renowned artists of his day to realize his plans: the painters Gilg Sesselschreiber, Jörg Kölderer, Ulrich Tiefenbrunn, Albrecht Dürer, Jörg Polhamer the Elder and Christian Amberger;

Portrait of Emperor Maximilian I by Bernhard Strigel (1460 – 1528)

Cymbarka of Mazovia, Grandmother of Emperor Maximilian I

Mary of Burgundy, first Wife of Emperor Maximilian I

the sculptors Veit Stoss, Hans Leinberger and Leonhard Magt; the casters Peter and Georg Löffler, Gilg Sesselschreiber and Stefan Godl. By 1519, the year of the emperor's death, only a fraction of the planned statues had been completed. The remains of Maximilian I are not in Innsbruck, but rather in the Palace Chapel (Burgkapelle) in Wiener Neustadt, where he was brought in accordance with his will after his death in Wels, Upper Austria. Nevertheless, the (empty) tomb of Emperor Maximilian with the famous, larger-than-life bronze figures constitutes one of Tyrol's most important monuments. The figures are known as the ★**"Schwarze Mannder," or "Black Statues."** Work on the figures was continued under Ferdinand I and his son Ferdinand II, and after nearly 80 years in the making, the work was completed: 28 large figures and 23 statuettes (20 busts are housed in Ambras Castle, one in a Munich museum) stand guard on both sides of the **sarcophagus** (or cenotaph), which was designed between 1560 and 1580 by the Cologne artist F. Abel, the Court Painter in Prague. It is made of various sorts of marble and its four sides hold 24 magnificent alabaster reliefs depicting scenes from Maximilian's life (battles, his wedding, his coronation). The figure on the lid of the sarcophagus, the kneeling emperor and the "four cardinal virtues" are the work of Alexander Colin. The sarcophagus is surrounded by a splendid **Renaissance grille,** which the Court

Locksmith of Prague, Jörg Schmidhammer, made between 1568 and 1573. As the site of the largest and most significant tomb of an emperor north of the Alps, the Court Church is particularly impressive. Further objects of note within the church: the **high altar,** erected in 1755 according to the plans of the Viennese Court Architect Nikolaus Pacassi; the magnificent **Sovereign's Choir (Fürstenchor)** on the upper floor, decorated with beautiful inlays; the **organ,** made by Jörg Ebert in 1558 and still played to this day; a carved coat of arms of Emperor Ferdinand I, held up by griffins in the center of the organ. The **tombs of the Tyrolean Freedom Fighters** of 1809, Andreas Hofer, Joseph Speckbacher and Brother Joachim Haspinger, are also found here.
A flight of stairs leads to the **Silver Chapel (Silberne Kapelle).**

Archduke Ferdinand II, the art patron who also erected Ambras Castle, had the Silver Chapel built as a place of burial for himself and his wife, Philippine Welser, between 1578 and 1587 by Hans Lucchese and son. The altar is especially noteworthy. It is made of ebony and ivory and has a silver relief (works of the Innsbruck Court Goldsmith Anton Ort) from which the chapel derives its name. On the left-hand side stands the famous cedarwood organ, an important Italian Renaissance piece from the 16th century. To this day, concerts are often given on it.

A combined ticket es available for admission to the Court Church and the Museum of Tyrolean Folk Art.

The former **New Monastery (Neues Stift)** adjoins the Court Church to the east. It was built from 1553 to 1561 under Emperor Ferdinand I and put at the disposal of the Franciscan Order. Niclas Türing designed the magnificent cloister in 1561. In 1719, the building acquired the lovely Baroque façade based on designs by Georg Anton Gumpp. During the years 1775 to 1785, it contained the "Theresianische Ritterakademie" and between 1868 and 1910 it served as a high school. It has been home to the **Museum of Tyrolean Folk Art (Tiroler Volkskunstmuseum; see Museums)** since 1924.

◄ ***To this day, the Ebert organ sounds beautiful when played***

Joan the Mad
(1479 – 1555)
Wife of Philip the Handsom
Daughter-in-law of Maximil
Heiress to the Habsburg dc

Ferdinand the Catholic of Spain
(1452 – 1516)
Father of Joan the Mad

Kunigunde
(1465 – 1520)
Sister of Maximilian

Elisabeth of Gorizia-Tyrol
(1263 – 1313)
Wife of Albert I

Mary of Burgundy
(1457 – 1482)
First Wife of Maximilian

Elisabeth of Hungary
(deceased 1443)
Wife of Albert II (V)

Godfrey of Bouillon
(1061 – 1100)
King of Jerusalem

King Albert I
(1248 – 1308)
Son of Rudolf I of Habsburg

Frederick IV (with the Empty Purse)
(1382 – 1439)
Great-Uncle of Maximilian

Leopold III the Virtuous
(1351 – 1386)
Great-Grandfather of Maximilian

Albert IV of Habsburg
(deceased 1240)
Father of Rudolf I

Leopold III the Holy of Babenberg
(1073 – 1136)

Emperor Frederick III
(1415 – 1493)
Father of Maximilian

King Albert II (V)
(1397 – 1433)

Entran

ILIAN I (1459 – 1519)

hilip the Good of Burgundy
1396 – 1467)
ather of Charles the Bold

Charles the Bold
(1433 – 1477)
First Father-in-law of Maximilian

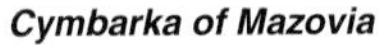

Cymbarka of Mazovia
(deceased 1429)
Grandmother of Maximilian

Margret of Austria
(1480 – 1530)
Daughter of Maximilian

Bianca Maria Sforza
(1472 – 1511)
Second Wife of Maximilian

Sigismund the Rich
(1427 – 1496)
Uncle and Adoptive Father of Maximilian

King Arthur of England
(deceased 537)

John of Portugal
(deceased 1385)
Ancestor of Maximilian's Mother

Ernest (the Iron Duke) of Austria
(1377 – 1424)
Grandfather of Maximilian

Theodorich, King of the Goths
(454 – 562)

Albert II the Wise
(1298 – 1358)
Grandson of Rudolf of Habsburg

King Rudolf I of Habsburg
(1218 – 1291)
Founder of the Habsburg dynasty

King Philip the Handsome
(1478 – 1506)
Son of Maximilian

King Clovis I
(466 – 511)
Founder of the Frankish kingdom

This plan was taken from the guide "Hofkirche, Maximiliansgrabmal, Silberne Kapelle – Innsbruck," published by the Museum of Tyrolean Folk Art.

Hungerburg – Pfarrkirche zur hl. Theresia (Hungerburg – Parish Church of St. Theresa)

The parish church was designed by Siegfried Thurner and built in 1932. Ernst Nepo painted a fresco of St. Theresa above the entrance in 1935; the frescoes inside are also his work. Max Weiler, at present the most highly regarded modern artist in Tyrol, painted the following murals in 1946: "Homage to the Sacred Heart," "Mount of Olives," "The Last Supper" and "Crucifixion." Some of these murals are highly controversial.

This fresco by the Tyrolean artist Max Weiler was controversial for many years

Igls – Pfarrkirche zum hl. Aegidius und den 14 Nothelfern (Igls - Parish Church of St. Giles and the 14 Auxiliary Saints)

This house of prayer was first mentioned in a document in 1286. The originally Gothic single-nave building was baroqued around 1700. The murals and ceiling frescoes are attributed to Joseph Schmutzer (1777). The high altar painting dates back to 1781; it depicts St. Giles and is the work of Johann Baptist Lampi the Elder. The side statues are of St. Blaise and St. Erasmus. Have a look inside the funerary chapel adjoining the northern side of the parish church: the Late Gothic fresco of the Crucifixion is worth seeing. The remarkable wrought-iron grave crosses in the churchyard are of interest, too.

Jesuitenkirche zur hl. Dreifaltigkeit (Jesuit Church of the Holy Trinity)

This church was designed by the Court Master Builder Christoph Gumpp the Younger and erected on Universitätsstrasse between the Old University and the Old University Library from 1627 to 1646. It was a gift of Leopold V and his wife Claudia de Medici. Relatively recently, in 1901, the façade was endowed with gables and towers. The church was badly damaged by bombing in 1943. The altar in the right-hand nave is dedicated to St. Peter Canisius, one of Tyrol's patron saints. In 1959, the Tyrolean Rifle Company donated the Sacred Heart Bell. Cast by the Innsbruck Grassmayr company, the bell weighs 9,600 kilograms and is the second-largest bell in Austria; only the Pummerin in Vienna's St. Stephen's Cathedral surpasses it in size. Archduchess Claudia commissioned the crypt (Fürstengruft) with intersecting vaults in 1636; her husband, Archduke Leopold V (deceased 1632), she herself (deceased 1648) and four other Habsburg sovereigns are buried here. The tombs of members of the Jesuit Order are found in the adjoining rooms. Since the history of the Jesuit Order is closely tied to that of the university, see the description of the latter for further details. The building of the Jesuit Theological College was constructed in the 19th century.

Kongresshaus (Congress Center)

A comedy theater was built on this location from 1628 to 1629, having been designed for Archduke Ferdinand Karl by the Court Master Builder Christoph Gumpp the Younger. In the 17th and 18th centuries, it served as the Court Riding School and housed the university library during the reign of Maria Theresa. During the Bavarian occupation (1806–1814), it was converted into a toll station, whence the name "Dogana," which is still used for one of the large halls. The building fell into disrepair in the 19th and 20th centuries and bombing attacks in 1944 demolished all but its outer walls. The Innsbruck architect Hubert Prachensky designed and built the modern congress center from 1970 to 1973, integrating what remained of the old structure. Expansion and renovation of the building followed from 1993 to 1995.

Landestheater (Tyrolean State Theater)

Archduke Ferdinand Karl had the Court Theater built between 1653 and 1655. The building standing here today was built in its place from 1844 to 1864 in the Neo-Classical style; it was designed by Giuseppe Segusini. The four

Corinthian columns at the main entrance are of special note. Franz Pöhacker made the bronze reliefs in the foyer; the mosaics are the

Leopold V on horseback; in the background, the Court Church and the Court Palace

work of Richard K. Fischer.
The **Leopold Fountain (Leopoldsbrunnen)** was built in 1621 and stands in the garden between the Tyrolean State Theater and a smaller stage known as the

One of the figures on the edge of the Leopold Fountain

Kammerspiele. It is named after Archduke Leopold V, Sovereign of Tyrol, who had it built. Caspar Gras designed the models for the bronze statues, which were cast by Heinrich and Friedrich Reinhardt. Oceanus, Diana, Amphitrite and a nymph sit on the fountain edge. The equestrian statue of Leopold V can be seen atop the fountain.

Landhaus (Tyrolean House of Parliament)

The Court Master Builder Georg Anton Gumpp built the three-storied **Old House of Parliament (Altes Landhaus)** between 1725 and 1728. It is regarded as one of Innsbruck's most magnificent Baroque buildings. The stairs leading up to the second and third floors are superb. Statues and busts of the gods stand in the niches on the side walls. Marvellous stuccowork adorns the ceilings. The **Assembly Room (Landtags-Sitzungssaal)** is reached through the carved doors. The beautiful frescoes on the walls and ceiling depict scenes from the Old Testament set in the Tyrolean landscape; Cosmas Damian Asam painted them in 1734. Carved white statues stand in the round niches; they are the work of Nikolaus Moll and portray Emperor Leopold I and Archduke Leopold V, among other important persons.

Georg Anton Gumpp also built the **House of Parliament Chapel (Landhauskapelle)** of St. George from 1725 to 1728.

The **New State Capital Building (Neues Landhaus)** is connected with the Old House of Parliament and the Fugger-Taxis Palace (Palais Fugger-Taxis) and was erected in 1938.

The **Freedom Monument (Freiheitsdenkmal)** dominates **Eduard Wallnöfer Square (Eduard-Wallnöfer-Platz,** also called Landhausplatz). Pascard, a Frenchman, designed it in 1948. The iron coats of arms of the nine Austrian states were wrought by Anton Fritz; Emmerich Kerle cast the bronze eagle.

The Church of Our Lady of Perpetual Help

Mariahilfkirche (Church of Our Lady of Perpetual Help)

The Estates of Tyrol had this parish church built on Mariahilfstrasse between 1647 and 1649 out of gratitude for averting danger during the Thirty Years War; it was designed by Christoph Gumpp the Younger. The church consists of a central building with a tall dome and adjoining, semi-circular chapels. Kaspar Waldmann painted the ceiling frescoes in the narthex in 1689; the marvellous grille is the work of Adam Neyer (1731). The high altar is crowned by a copy of Lucas Cranach's famous painting of Our Lady of Perpetual Help.

Neues Rathaus (New City Hall)

In the 18th century, three Gothic buildings were combined to form the Palais Künigl. This structure acquired a façade in 1848. The Baroque columns in the ground-floor entrance used to support an oriel. A simple Baroque fountain stands in the courtyard.

Ottoburg

The Ottoburg, now covered with wild grape vines, was commissioned by Emperor Maximilian I in the 15th century. It was constructed next to the former city wall, remnants of which are still visible, and within the borders of the former Andechs fortress. It is named after the last count in the Andechs line, Otto VIII. The red and white shutters enliven the gray, heavily segmented façade. The building's ownership as well as its function changed often. For many years now, it has housed an excellent restaurant with wine bar. The dining rooms with intersecting and stellar vaults are worth seeing. The Ottoburg is the oldest building still standing on Herzog-Friedrich-Strasse.
In front of the Ottoburg, facing the Inn River, stands a monument bearing the inscription "Father and Son." It was made by Christian Plattner to commemorate the Freedom Fighters of 1809.

Palais Fugger-Taxis (Fugger-Taxis Palace)

This palace stands next to the **Old House of Parliament,** to which it has been connected by way of another building since 1905. The palace was erected by Johann Martin Gumpp the Elder between 1679 and 1680 for Count Hans Otto Fugger. It is Innsbruck's oldest Baroque palace designed in the Italian style. A magnificent façade facing the street embellishes the main structure; two wings enclose a courtyard with a lovely garden. In 1702, the building came into the hands of the counts of Welsberg. In 1784, the counts of Thurn und Taxis acquired it, using it as a post office. The State of Tyrol acquired the building in 1905, and it now houses, among other things, an art gallery. The Late Neo-Classical ceiling frescoes by Martin Knoller in the Paris Room (Parissaal) are especially worth admiring, as are the Rococo wall decorations in the same room, made in 1750 and discovered in 1921 in the course of restoration work.

Rudolfsbrunnen (Rudolf Fountain)

The fountain was erected on Bozner Platz in 1877 to celebrate the 500th anniversary of Tyrol becoming an Austrian domain (1363-1863). It was designed by Friedrich Schmidt. The larger-than-life bronze statue of Rudolf IV stands atop the fountain pedestal, which is decorated with coats of arms.

St. Nikolaus Pfarrkirche (Parish Church of St. Nicholas)

Documents reveal that a Gothic church was consecrated on this site as far back as 1502. A new building was constructed between 1882 and 1884, based on plans by Vienna's cathedral architect, Friedrich von Schmidt. It is the most important Gothic Revival church in Tyrol. This triple-nave hall church (all three naves of equal height) has intersecting vaults and a transept. The furnishings are uniformly Gothic Revival. Friedrich von Schmidt also designed the high altar. The reliefs at the side altars and near the pulpit are the work of Josef Bachlechner the Elder, who also designed the stations of the cross. The richly colored stained glass windows, made around 1900, are especially powerful.

★ Schloss Ambras (Ambras Castle)

The castle stands in the southeast of the city on a plateau. It is unclear when the first fortress was built on this site. It is known, however, that it served as the residence of the powerful counts of Andechs in the 11th and 12th centuries. In connection with a dispute, Henry the Proud of Bavaria seized and destroyed the fortress in 1132. Although rebuilt shortly thereafter, it no longer carried the same weight for the counts of Andechs, who had already erected another fortress in their newly founded city of "Inspruck" (see Ottoburg). When the counts of Andechs died out in 1248, the fortress came into the hands of the counts of Tyrol, who gave it to various nobles as feudal tenure. Innsbruck and Ambras Castle both gained considerable significance under Duke Sigismund the Rich. During this period, in 1465, the fortress chapel was newly consecrated. The small, beautiful altar of St. George from the period of Emperor Maximilian I was carved around 1510 by Sebald Bocksdorfer. The chapel was renovated in the Gothic Revival style in the 19th century. When Archduke Ferdinand II became sovereign of Tyrol, he chose Ambras as his residence. He made a gift of the fortress to his wife, Philippine Welser, in 1564 and had it rebuilt as a splendid Renaissance castle. Archduke Ferdinand II drafted the renovation plans in Prague and entrusted his Court Architect from Italy, Hans Lucchese, with the project's realization. The roof of the **main building** is decorated with many chimneys, which vary greatly in form and color. The sovereign's family had approximately 40 rooms at its disposal. Even today, the fully preserved bathroom is interesting to see. The dining-room ceiling, painted in 1584 with astronomical motifs, is also fascinating. The Portrait Gallery of Austrian History from 1400 to 1800 is located in one of the rooms; this priceless art-historic collection contains 200 paintings by Dutch, German, Austrian, Italian, French and Spanish artists. The Court Painter Heinrich Teufel adorned the courtyard with Renaissance frescoes. The **Spanish Hall** was built by Hans Lucchese from 1570 to 1571 beneath the castle's main building to serve as an assembly room. It is 43 meters long, 10 meters wide and 5 meters tall. An Italian artist painted the portraits of the 26 Tyrolean sovereigns – from Albert I to Ferdinand II (approximately from the 13th to the 16th centuries).

The coffered ceiling, made by Court Cabinetmaker Konrad Gottlieb in 1571, and the splendidly inlaid doors are very impressive. The Ambras Castle Concerts (Ambraser Schlosskonzerte) and the Festival Weeks of Early Music (Festwochen der Alten Musik) take place here in the summer months. Under Ferdinand II and his wife, the castle became a center of European court life and culture. It developed into a favorite gathering place for artists, scholars and noblemen. After the early death of his wife in 1580, Archduke Ferdinand II devoted himself to his passion for collecting, which brought him great fame. He owned a valuable library containing, among other treasures, the Ambras Book of Heroes (Ambraser Heldenbuch) with the only existing copy of The Song of Gudrun (Gudrunlied); this book is now in the National Library in Vienna. Above all, he loved his collection of armor once worn by famous contemporaries. Last but not least, he established a Room of Art Works and Curiosities; the pieces in this collection are still highly valued. Many of the treasures he collected are found in the Museum of Fine Art in Vienna (Kunsthistorisches Museum; see Museum of Fine Art), but Ambras Castle is still home to a large number of impressive artworks.

Duke Sigismund the Rich

During the two and a half centuries following the death of Ferdinand II in 1595, the castle structure remained unaltered. After the Habsburg line in Tyrol died out in 1665, large portions of the collections were transfered to Vienna (some of the objects were later brought back). For many years, the castle served as a military hospital. It was restored once again in 1850. The successor to the throne, Archduke Franz Ferdinand, had been planning since 1907 to make the castle his summer residence. These plans were never realized: the Archduke was assassinated in Sarajevo in 1914. From 1918 on, the building was restored to its former grandeur. The castle's collections have been open to the public since 1926. The Ambras Castle Concerts and the Festival Weeks of Early Music (see Spanish Hall and Concerts) have breathed new life into this former cultural center.

The beautiful **castle park,** replete with waterfall and ponds, is the perfect place to relax and stroll.

Ambras Castle draws art lovers from far and wide

The 16th-century Spanish Hall with its magnificent coffered ceiling and portraits of Tyrolean sovereigns

Servitenkirche und -kloster zum hl. Josef (Servite Church and Convent of St. Joseph)

Katharina Gonzaga, second wife of Archduke Ferdinand II, had this church and convent built in 1614. Both buildings burned down in 1620 but were soon rebuilt. In 1722, they were baroqued. Between 1817 and 1820, the interiors were refurnished. The altar painting depicting the marriage of the Virgin Mary is particularly lovely; painted in 1628, it is the Innsbruck Court Painter Martin Theophil Pollack's masterpiece. The tabernacle in the Peregrini Chapel is also admirable; stained black and decorated with ivory, it dates back to around 1620. The sacristy, library and **Art Room (Kunstkammer,** see Museums) are reached through the vaulted cloister. A Late Gothic stone relief is found above the inside of the convent door.

Tower of the Servite Church

Spitalskirche zum hl. Geist (Hospital Church of the Holy Spirit)

The church was first documented in 1326. The Court Master Builder Johann Martin Gumpp the Elder designed the new building between 1700 and 1701. The long, eastern side of the church was integrated into the building façades along Maria-Theresien-Strasse. The only remaining original fresco is the Cecelia Fresco by Johann Josef Waldmann (1702); it was exposed above the organ gallery in 1962. The other frescoes were painted by Hans Andre (1962). There are numerous articles of interest in the church's

The Hospital Church, renovated in 1994

interior: the stuccolustro high altar by Christoph Benedetti (1705), the Late Gothic crucifix, the stuccolustro pulpit by Franz Roilo (1965) and the organ with its stuccolustro casing.

★ Sprungschanze am Bergisel (Ski Jump at Bergisel)

From the parking lot on Bergisel, you can walk to the ski jump in a matter of minutes. The ski jumping events of the 1964 and 1976 Winter Olympic Games took place here. The arena holds approximately 50,000 spectators. The two torches, where the Olympic fire burned during the games, stand at the end of the landing area, from where there is a marvellous view of the city and the Nordkette mountains to the north. Bronze plaques record the names of all the medal winners. If you have athletic ambitions, be sure to climb to the take-off platform; your efforts will be rewarded with the magnificent panorama.

Each year in early January, one event of the Intersport Ski Jumping Tournament (Vier-Schanzen-Tournee) is held here. The stadium is also used for other events, such as open-air concerts. In 1988, a large diocesan celebration took place here with Pope John Paul II.

Winners of the 90-meter ski jumping event:

1964: *1. Veikko Kankkonen (SF)*
2. Toralf Engan (N)
3. Torgeir Brandtzaeg (N)

1976: *1. Karl Schnabl (A)*
2. Anton Innauer (A)
3. Henry Glass (former GDR)

Wilten Abbey Church with the Nordkette mountains

Stiftskirche zum hl. Laurentius und Praemonstratenser-Chorherren-Stift in Wilten (Wilten Abbey Church of St. Lawrence and Premonstratensian Abbey)

Legend has it that the founding of this abbey has its roots in the remorse felt by the giant Haymon after having slain the giant Thyrsus. This is said to have occurred between the sixth and the ninth centuries. The patronage of St. Lawrence implies that this was probably an early Christian cult site. The **abbey church** retained its Romanesque form into the 17th century, despite several renovations and remodelings. During the search for the bones of the giant Haymon, the church caved in; it was decided that it should be completely rebuilt. Christoph Gumpp the Younger designed the new building, which was constructed between 1651 and 1655. The adjoining abbey was also renovated from 1670 to 1696 in accordance with his designs. The façade was created by Georg Anton Gumpp in 1716. The two statues of the giants Haymon and Thyrsus on either side of the main entrance were made by Nikolaus Moll during the same period. In 1939, the abbey was closed; the church, together with the other buildings, served as a furniture warehouse. In 1944, the buildings were heavily damaged by fire bombing. The makeshift restoration from 1946 to 1955 necessitated an additional renovation in the 1980s.

The church's interior corresponds with that of Southern German pilaster churches. A Late Gothic fan vault is found behind the high altar. Between 1702 and 1707, Kaspar Waldmann painted the richly colored ceiling frescoes: in the choir, the Coronation of the Virgin Mary; in the nave, the Virgin Mary handing a monastic garb to St. Norbert, the founder of the Premonstratensian Order. Those frescoes of Waldmann destroyed in World War II were replaced with new ones by Hans Andre in 1962. Within the church, our attention is also captured by the enormous high altar, made by the Court Cabinetmaker Paul Huber in 1655. The high altar painting (Blessed Virgin as Queen of the Rosary in the Company of Angels, St. Lawrence and St. Stephen) is by Egid Schor (1671). The organ was built in the 17th century and is especially precious; it is the work of Daniel Herz, an organ builder from Wilten. The large new organ was built in 1963. The five black and gold altars in the side chapels of the nave date back to about 1670. The chapel of St. John (Johanneskapelle) was donated by the Trautson family (their tomb slab is found here). The Chapel of St. Anne (Annenkapelle) contains a fresco depicting Wilten and Innsbruck being protected by St. Anne during the Bavarian invasion (see St. Anne's Column) with a fascinating view of the city. The Chapel of St. Norbert (Norbertikapelle) holds the crypt of the abbots of Wilten from Gregor Stremer to 1906. In the Chapel of the Holy Cross (Kreuzkapelle), our attention turns to a precious, Late Gothic crucifix. In the vestibule, we find a beautiful rosette grille by Adam Neyer of Innsbruck (1707) as well as an enormous carved Gothic statue of the giant Haymon. Premonstratensian monks have resided in the adjoining **abbey building** since 1138. It has several noteworthy rooms; **St. Norbert's Room (Norbertisaal),** formerly known as the Emperor's Room, is the most representative of these. Concerts and special events are often held here. In 1710, it was decorated

The Giant Haymon stands guard beside the main entrance

The façade of Wilten Abbey Church in the glow of the setting sun

with Early Rococo stuccowork and ceiling frescoes by Kaspar Waldmann portraying the life of St. Norbert, the Order's founder. The **Altmutter Room (Altmuttersaal)** is adorned with a magnificent coffered ceiling, an 18th-century patterned parquet floor and wall coverings depicting fantasy landscapes and exotic animals by Franz Altmutter from the early 19th century. The hunting scenes, painted in 1712 by Kaspar Waldmann and decorating the walls of the **Hunting Room (Jagdzimmer),** are certainly worth seeing. Beautiful frescoes painted by the circle of artists around Michael Pacher have been exposed in the Chapter Room (Kapitelsaal). In the same room there is a winged altarpiece made in 1491, a gift of Duke Sigismund to the Church of St. Sigismund in the Sellrain Valley. The shrine holds figures of St. Sigismund, St. Agnes and St. Notburga; interesting paintings adorn its wings. Kaspar Waldmann's paintings hang in the **refectory;** originally Gothic, this room was renovated in 1708. The **library** counts numerous precious books and manuscripts in its collection. The **Abbey Museum (Stiftsmuseum;** see Museums) is worth visiting.

Many gravestones from the crypt are displayed in the **cloister.** The oldest dates back to 1300.

For many centuries, Wilten Abbey was of great cultural significance. As early as the 12th century, it ran a highly regarded Latin school, commissioned many artworks and carried out important pastoral work. The Premonstratensian monks are responsible for colonizing the Sellrain Valley, which belonged to the abbey. In the 17th and 18th centuries, several monks taught at the University of Innsbruck. In fact, until 1918 the abbots held a seat in the Tyrolean Estates.

Tiroler Landesmuseum Ferdinandeum (Tyrolean State Museum Ferdinandeum)

The building was constructed between 1842 and 1845 in accordance with designs by Anton Mutschlechner. Originally two-storied, an extra floor was added in 1884 along with a new façade (see Museums).

"Portrait of an Old Man" by Rembrandt van Rijn

Maria Theresa had the Arch of Triumph decorated with figures and reliefs

Triumphpforte (Arch of Triumph)

This triple-arched monument at the southern end of Maria-Theresien-Strasse was modeled on Roman triumphal arches. Maria Theresa had it refashioned to mark the occasion of the marriage of her son Leopold (later Emperor Leopold II) to the Spaniard Maria Ludovica. The square stone blocks were originally part of the demolished Gate of St. George (Georgstor). They are made of sturdy breccia from Hötting. Balthasar Moll made the marble reliefs in 1774. Those on the south side commemorate the marriage; those on the north side remind us of the death of Leopold's father, Emperor Francis I, who passed away at the wedding in Innsbruck.

University

The university was founded on Herrengasse in Innsbruck in 1669 under Emperor Leopold I. The **Old University** adjoins the east side of the Museum of Tyrolean Folk Art. The building housing the Old University originally served as the Jesuit Theological College, founded in 1556. Emperor Ferdinand I brought a number of Jesuits to Innsbruck in 1561 to counteract the Reformation. Johann Martin Gumpp the Elder added the harmonious façade in the 16th century, incorporating the former Jesuit College (Old University Library). In 1776, after the Jesuits had been expelled from Innsbruck, a lack of space caused the university to move from Herrengasse to the newly vacated buildings. The Jesuits returned to Innsbruck in 1838 and many are active at the university. The Theological Faculty is still located on Universitätsstrasse. The various rooms there are worth a visit; for instance, the Leopold Room (Leopoldssaal) has a lovely stucco ceiling. The adjoining building housed the departments of

Geology, Mineralogy and Botany into the 1980s. Construction of the Neo-Baroque **New University** and **University Library** on Innrain was begun in 1914; the doors of the New University opened in 1924. Modern buildings followed from 1980 to 1986 to create more space for the humanities and natural sciences.

The **Gumpp family** brought forth gifted master builders, carpenters, painters and copper engravers, who produced numerous works of art in Tyrol and Bavaria in the 17th and 18th centuries. **Christoph Gumpp the Younger** (1600 – 1672) was one of the most important members of the family. He designed the comedy theater (the congress center stands in its place today, see Kongresshaus), Innsbruck's Mariahilfkirche (see above), and the Stiftskirche Wilten (see above). He was appointed Court Master Builder in 1633. Of his 19 children from two marriages, six were to become artists. One of them, **Johann Martin Gumpp the Elder** (1643 – 1729) designed the Palais Fugger-Taxis (see above) and the Spitalskirche (see above). In 1672, he succeeded his deceased father as Court Master Builder. **Georg Anton Gumpp** (1682 – 1754) and **Johann Martin Gumpp the Younger** (1686-1765) were his sons. Georg Anton Gumpp designed the façade of the Stiftskirche Wilten and that of the New Monastery (now the Museum of Tyrolean Folk Art) on Universitätsstrasse. He also built the Old House of Parliament (see above) and St. John's Church (Johanneskirche) on Innrain. In addition, Johann Martin Gumpp the Younger played a major part in rebuilding Innsbruck's Court Palace (see Hofburg). His death brought to an end the enormous artistic influence, which this family exerted on Innsbruck's architecture. **Gumppstrasse** in Pradl was named in the family's honor.

Please consult the map inside the back cover.

The following tour of the city guides you to the most interesting and prominent sights in the inner city. A detailed description of the sights in bold print can be found in the Chapter "Sights from A to Z" (pages 13 – 44).

Our tour starts at the **Arch Triumph (Triumphpforte),** seven minutes from the train station and close to bus stops and underground parking for cars. Look to the south for a view of **Bergisel** and Patscherkofel and turn north to admire the awesome Nordkette. From here, begin walking north on Maria-Theresien-Strasse past the **Fugger-Taxis Palace (Palais Fugger-Taxis)** and the **Old House of Parliament (Landhaus)** on the right and the **Servite Church (Servitenkirche)** on the left. After crossing Meranerstrasse/Anichstrasse, take a look at the famous **St. Anne's Column (Annasäule)** in the center of the street. Musicians and artists from around the world often congregate around the column, bringing the picturesque street to life. At the end of Maria-Theresien-Strasse, cross Marktgraben/Burggraben, where the city wall once enclosed the southern part of the city, and head toward the **Golden Roof (Goldenes Dachl)** on Herzog-Friedrich-Strasse. Stop and take in the handsome **15th- and 16th-century buildings** with their oriels and arcades. There are lots of shops including souvenir shops, inns and cafés on the ground level. If the weather is nice, sit down and take a break at one of the many outdoor cafés and try the different pastries, enjoy a quiet cup of coffee, or have some ice cream and catch a little of the activity in the Old City. After you're rested, take a look at the Golden Roof close up. It's hard to miss, staked out with a year-round cast of tour groups harking the polyglot commentaries of their colorful guides. Turn left and continue along Herzog-Friedrich-Strasse, passing the Gasthof Goldener Adler, one of the oldest (and more expensive) inns in Innsbruck. Near the entrance is a plaque "immortalizing" all the famous people, who have stayed at this inn. Further down the street is the **Ottoburg** and the memorial to the Tyrolean Freedom Fighters. Cross Herzog-Otto-Strasse and you will suddenly be at the Inn River, from which the city takes its name.

Many prominent people have stayed at the Hotel Goldener Adler

From here you have a spectacular view of the colorful rows of houses across the river in Mariahilf and Hötting. Walk downriver a bit, make a right turn onto the first small street (Badgasse) and pass the Innsbruck Municipal Archives (Stadtarchiv). This street leads to

Picturesque hustle and bustle under the City Tower

Domplatz with the magnificent **St. James Cathedral (Dom zu St. Jakob).** The path to the right of the Cathedral leads to the **Court Palace (Hofburg)** on Rennweg with the **Tyrolean State Theater (Tiroler Landestheater)** across the street. To the right, next to the Franciscan Arch (Franziskanerbogen), are the Court Church (Hofkirche) and the Tyrolean Museum of Folk Art (Tiroler Volkskunstmuseum), connected to the church on the east side. Go east down Universitätsstrasse to Karl-Rahner-Platz (Karl Rahner Square) in front of the University Church or **Jesuit Church (Jesuitenkirche),** between the buildings housing the School of Theology. Take the passageway to the right of the church to reach Prof.-Franz-Mair-Gasse and the **Tyrolean State Museum Ferdinandeum (Tiroler Landesmuseum Ferdinandeum).** Cross Museumstrasse here and walk south. Follow Wilhelm-Greil-Strasse to Bozner Platz with the **Rudolf Fountain (Rudolfsbrunnen)** on the left. Continue along Wilhelm-Greil-Strasse to the **Old House of Parliament (Landhaus).** Pass the imposing memorial on Eduard Wallnöfer Square (Eduard-Wallnöfer-Platz or Landhausplatz) and return to the tour's starting point. The walking time for this tour (without stopping to view the churches, museums etc.) is approximately two hours.

The richly colored houses of Mariahilf are some of the oldest in Innsbruck ▸▸

Adolf-Pichler-Platz: As captain of the academic division of the Tyrolean Rifle Company, Adolf Pichler (1819 – 1900) fought against the Italians. He later served as university professor of geology and mineralogy in Innsbruck. A recognized Tyrolean folk poet, he was awarded one of the city's highest honors.

Anichstrasse: Peter Anich (1723 – 1766), certainly the most famous Tyrolean cartographer, lived and worked in nearby Oberperfuss. Among other projects, he drew up at Empress Maria Theresa's request a map of North and South Tyrol (Atlas Tyrolensis), a very precise cartographic work for its day.

"Peter Anich" – portrait by Philipp Haller from 1759, oil painting in the cartography section of the Tyrolean State Museum – Zeughaus

Andreas-Hofer-Strasse: Andreas Hofer (1767 – 1810) is renowned as the leader of Tyrol's patriotic uprising in 1809 (see Bergisel and Hofkirche).

Blasius-Hueber-Strasse: Blasius Hueber (1735 – 1814), the most important assistant cartographer to Peter Anich (see Anichstrasse), continued work on the "Atlas Tyrolensis" after the latter's death.

Colingasse: Alexander Colin (1526 – 1612) was a Flemish sculptor whose works include the reliefs on Emperor Maximilian I's tomb (see Hofkirche).

Cranachstrasse: Lucas Cranach the Elder (1472 – 1533), a well-known artist from Upper Franconia, painted the famous "Our Lady of Perpetual Help" for Innsbruck's St. James Cathedral (see Dom).

Erzherzog-Eugen-Strasse: Archduke Eugene (1863 – 1954), an Austro-Hungarian field marshal, commanded the Austrian army (1915 – 1918) against Italy during World War I. In 1945 he made Igls his home and is buried in the Cathedral (see Dom).

Fennerstrasse: Franz Fenner von Fennberg (1759 – 1824) was a field marshal and founded the Tyrolean Rifle (Kaiserjäger) Regiment (see Bergisel).

Gilmstrasse: Hermann von Gilm (1812 – 1864) was the greatest Tyrolean lyric poet of his time.

Grassmayrstrasse: Johann Georg Grassmayr (1695 – 1751) was a painter whose works include the altar painting in the Basilica of Wilten (see Basilika Wilten). He was a member of the famous bell-making family (see Glockenmuseum).

Haspingerstrasse: The Capuchin monk Joachim Haspinger (1776 – 1858) fought at the side of Andreas Hofer and Josef Speckbacher in the uprising of 1809.

Haymongasse: Legend has it that the giant Haymon was the founder of Wilten Abbey (see Stift Wilten).

Herzog-Friedrich-Strasse: Duke Frederick (1382 – 1439), the sovereign of Tyrol, was popularly known as "Freddy with the Empty Purse." After ruling Tyrol jointly with his brother Leopold until 1406, he became its sole ruler. He came into disgrace when he supported the claimant to the papal throne, who failed to be elected at the Council of Constance. Emperor Sigismund declared him an outlaw and he was banished from the Council. Although he submitted to the Emperor in 1415, he was arrested in Constance. The Tyroleans were loyal to him, and in 1416 he was able to escape. He hid in Rofenhöfen (2,011 m) high up in the Oetz Valley until 1418 when the Emperor and the Council made a formal peace with Tyrol. It was then that he received his nickname. A votive plaque in the Basilica of Wilten (see Basilika Wilten) commemorates his return home. A good ruler, he brought prosperity to Tyrol. In 1420 he moved the royal residence from Castle Tyrol in Meran to the new court (see Goldenes Dachl) in Innsbruck. His tomb is located in the Abbey Church of Stams. The street named after him is the main street of the Old City (pedestrian zone). Until 1765 a gate (Vorstadttor) led out of the Old City. The buildings in the style of the Inn-Salzach cities give the street its typical appearance. The four- and five-story houses built on narrow plots are characteristic of this style. Other features include: oriels, blind façades, staircases doubling as air shafts, and ground-floor arcades, sometimes also spacious vaults. The buildings on this street all date back to the 15th and 16th centuries.

★The following buildings deserve special note: **Katzunghaus** (No. 16), whose unique reliefs on the oriel depicting dancing, jousting and musical scenes are attributed to Gregor Türing. **Trautsonhaus** (No. 22) has two polygonal oriels with sandstone reliefs and the Trautson/Madruz family coat of arms. The famous **Helblinghaus** (No. 10) is situated on the corner and has a Rococo façade as well as oriels on the corner and front. The lavish stucco façade dates back to 1730 and is ascribed to Anton Gigl. This building is an excellent example of middle-class wealth in the Old City. Take special notice of the net vault in the ground-floor arcade. The building was completely renovated from 1979 to 1980. It is named after Hans Helbling, who ran a little café in it in 1833. In front of Trautsonhaus is a marble fountain; it is

Helblinghaus

made him a wealthy man. Neither of his two marriages produced a legitimate heir. In 1477 he moved the mint from Meran to Hall in Tirol where precious silver coins were minted, thus his nickname. He stepped down in 1490 in favor of the later emperor, Maximilian. Duke Sigismund had seven castles built in Tyrol: "Sigmundsried" (Ried in the Upper Inn Valley), "Sigmundsburg" (below Fern Pass), "Sigmundsfreud" (Barwies), "Sigmundslust" (Vomp), "Sigmundseck" (Finstermünz/Nauders), "Sigmundsruh" (or "Burg Freundsberg" Schwaz), and "Sigmundskron" (near Bolzano in South Tyrol). After his death in 1496, he was buried in the sovereigns' crypt in Stams Abbey.

the only **city fountain** preserved in its original location and reportedly dates from the 16th century.

Herzog-Otto-Strasse: Otto II, Count of Andechs-Meran built his castle in the early 13th century where the Viktor Dankl Barracks were closed in 1985 (now the Tyrolean State School Authority). He also renewed and confirmed Innsbruck's city charter (1239).

Herzog-Sigmund-Ufer: Tyrol's Duke Sigismund (1427 – 1496) was nicknamed "the Rich." As the only son of Duke Frederick IV (see Herzog-Friedrich-Strasse), Sigismund at age 12 became the heir apparent under the tutelage of his cousin, later Frederick III (father of Emperor Maximilian I). In 1446 he took over full rule of Tyrol. At this time the lucrative silver mines in Schwaz began to flourish and

Kaiserjägerstrasse: This street commemorates the great valor of the Tyrolean Rifle Regiment in World War I.

Karl-Rahner-Platz: Karl Rahner (1904 – 1984) was a Jesuit priest and foremost theologian and philosopher at the universities of Innsbruck, Munich and Muenster.

Karl-Schönherr-Strasse: Karl Schönherr (1867 – 1943) of Axams was a doctor of medicine, author of numerous folk dramas and one of Austria's most famous playwrights.

Köldererstrasse: Jörg Kölderer (1480 – 1540) was a painter and architect at Emperor Maximilian's court. His works include the frescoes on the Golden Roof (see Goldenes Dachl) and the illustrations in the emperor's fishing journal.

Maria-Theresien-Strasse: Maria Theresa (1717 – 1780), wife of Emperor Francis I of Lorraine, ruled the Habsburg domains. The main street and favorite shopping venue bears her name. She visited Innsbruck to attend the marriage of her son in 1765 (see Triumphpforte and Hofburg).

Maximilianstrasse: Maximilian I (1459 – 1519) is indisputably Innsbruck and Tyrol's most important ruler. Before succeeding his close relative Duke Sigismund the Rich (see Herzog-Sigmund-Ufer) in 1490, he held the title of king of the Romans and regent of The Netherlands. He assumed the title of elected Holy Roman Emperor in 1508. From the outset Maximilian had strong ties to Tyrol and encouraged its cultural development. He benefited from the lucrative silver mines in Schwaz and always visited Tyrol to indulge in his greatest passion, hunting. Playing a clever hand at marriage politics, he fortified the power of the Habsburgs. In 1494 he married his second wife, Maria Bianca Sforza, in Innsbruck. This event spurred the renovation and reconstruction of the Golden Roof (see Goldenes Dachl). In 1500 he commissioned the "Zeughaus" (see Tiroler Landeskundliches Museum) and arranged for his tomb in the Court Church (see Hofkirche). In keeping with his last will he was buried in the Palace Chapel in Wiener Neustadt, the city where he was born.

Meinhardstrasse: Meinhard II (1237 – 1295) was born of the marriage between Meinhard I of Gorizia to Adelheid, daughter of Count Albert III of Tyrol (after the death of Albert III, Meinhard I and his brother-in-law ruled most of present-day Tyrol). Meinhard II ruled alone as of 1259; the settlement treaty of 1271 awarded him Tyrol, while his brother Albert received Gorizia. Meinhard II ruled from his residence in Meran (South Tyrol) and won other territories as well. As the sovereign of Tyrol, he successfully supported Rudolf of Habsburg against Otakar of Bohemia. In reciprocation he received Carinthia as a gift. After fire destroyed large parts of Innsbruck in 1292, Meinhard II had the Sill Canal built; it ran from Wilten through today's Meinhardstrasse and Sillgasse. Together with his wife, Elisabeth of Bavaria, he founded the Cistercian Monastery at Stams. He is buried there, in the family crypt of the Counts of Gorizia-Tyrol.

Philippine-Welser-Strasse: Philippine Welser (1527 - 1580), wife of Archduke Ferdinand II of Tyrol was mistress of Ambras Castle (see Schloss Ambras).

Rennweg: This was named after the former running (German: "rennen") and tournament square in front of the Court Palace.

Speckbacherstrasse: Josef Speckbacher (1767 – 1820) of Gnadenwald was a clever tactician in the Tyrolean Fight for Freedom of 1809 (see page 66).

Traklpark: Georg Trakl (1887 – 1914), a prominent lyric poet, spent much of his life in Innsbruck and published his works in the journal "Der Brenner." He is buried in the cemetery in Mühlau.

Gleirschjöchl with a storm coming on

Alpenvereinsmuseum (Alpine Club Museum)

Wilhelm-Greil-Strasse 15
Telephone: 59 5 47
Open: Mondays – Fridays 10 am – 5 pm
The museum documents the history of mountain climbing and the advent of alpinism to the Eastern Alps as well as the evolution of mountain-climbing equipment. Reliefs, paintings and cartographic exhibits are also worth seeing. One of the founders of the German Alpine Club in 1869 was the famous priest and alpinist Franz Senn; in 1873 it merged with the Austrian Alpine Club. Franz Senn brought alpinism to the Stubai and Oetz Valley Alps, where he carved trails, built shelters and trained mountain guides.

Bergisel- bzw. Kaiserjäger Museum (Bergisel Museum)

Bergisel 3
Telephone: 58 23 12
Open: Mar 1 – 31, 10 am – 3 pm, closed Mondays;
Apr 1 – Oct 31, daily 9 am – 5 pm
This museum commemorates the Battles of Bergisel in the Tyrolean Fight for Freedom. Vast collections of paintings, flags and weaponry recall the days of Andreas Hofer as well as the history of the Tyrolean Rifle (Kaiserjäger) Regiment, particularly its role in World War I. On the ground floor is the Memorial Chapel, which was built in 1959 to mark the 150th anniversary and which holds the "Book of Honor of Tyrol" containing the names of all Tyroleans who died in the line of duty between 1796 and 1945. Not far from Bergisel are the monuments commemorating the Tyrolean Fight for Freedom: the Andreas Hofer Monument and the chapel with the Tomb of Honor of the Kaiserjäger Regiment. The chapel's large windows offer a magnificent view of Innsbruck and the Nordkette.

★ Glockenmuseum (Bell Museum)

Leopoldstrasse 53
Telephone: 59 4 16
Open: Mondays – Fridays 9 am – 6 pm, Saturdays 9 am – 12 noon
For 14 generations the Grassmayr family has been casting bells for the entire world. Their 400 years of experience, history and tradition have brought them great success. The museum shows a bell's progress from iron ore to the finished product. In the casting room bell forms of clay are handcrafted, and in the Tone Room bell tones can be seen, heard and felt. You can view the bell makers go about their craft, making forms and casting bells.

Bell being cast

Hofburg (Court Palace)

Rennweg 1
Telephone: 58 71 86
Open: May 1 – Oct 31,
daily 9 am – 5 pm;
Nov 2 – Apr 30, Mondays – Saturdays 10 am – 5 pm (closed on holidays)
The late Gothic fortress constructed during the reign of Duke Sigismund "the Rich" was rebuilt under Maria Theresa between 1754 – 1770. Among the rooms on display are: the magnificent Giants' Room with ceiling frescoes by Franz Anton Maulpertsch, the Lorraine Room, the Andreas Hofer Room and the chapel.

Kaiserschützen-Museum (Imperial Rifle Regiment Museum)

Klostergasse 1
Telephone: 58 33 86
Open: May 2 – Sept 30, Mondays – Saturdays 10 am – 4 pm, Sundays 9 am – 12 noon
The museum documents the history of the Imperial Rifle Regiment from 1870 to 1918. The exhibit focuses on the defense of Tyrol against Italy in World War I. The museum also has a notable library.

★ Kunsthistorisches Museum - Sammlungen im Schloß Ambras(Museum of Fine Art – Collections in Ambras Castle)

Schloßstrasse 20
Telephone: 34 84 46
Open: Apr 1 – Oct 31, daily (except Tuesdays) 10 am – 5 pm
This Renaissance palace houses the oldest weaponry and armory collection in Europe and reflects Archduke Ferdinand II's (1529 –

Medieval knight's armor

1595) great passion as a collector. The Renaissance Spanish Hall with its portrait gallery is of particular interest, as is the beautifully landscaped park.

Kunstkammer im Servitenkloster (Art Room in the Servite Monastery)

Maria-Theresien-Strasse 42
Telephone: 58 88 83
Open: by appointment only
On display are sacred art objects, foremost of which being the memorial pieces from Archduke Ferdinand II's wife, Anna Katharina Gonzaga, the founder of the monastery, and paintings by Tyrolean artists of the 17th to 19th centuries.

Lokalbahnmuseum am alten Stubaitalbahnhof (Regional Train Museum at the old Stubai Tramway Terminal)

Pater-Reinisch-Weg 4
Telephone: 53 07 or 57 27 68
Open: May 1 – Oct 31, Saturdays 9 am – 5 pm
Approximately 200 illustrations and 14 historical rail vehicles recount the history of regional railroad and streetcar operations throughout Tyrol. By request you can arrange to take a special ride within Innsbruck on a historic streetcar.

Naturwissenschaftliche Sammlung (Natural Sciences Collection)

Feldstrasse 11a
Telephone: 58 72 86
A viewing of the numerous collections, including beetles and butterflies, can be arranged by prior appointment.

Olympia-Museum (Olympic Museum)

This museum documenting the 1964 and 1976 Winter Olympic Games in Innsbruck is leaving its original home at Herzog-Friedrich-Straße 15 (Golden Roof) and temporarily moving to Seefeld. Its permanent new home will be at the Bergisel Stadium with the 90-m ski jump, where the opening ceremony for the two winter Olympics was held and where the Olympic flame burned.

Rundgemälde der Schlacht am Bergisel (Panorama Painting of the Battle of Bergisel)

Rennweg 39
Telephone: 58 44 34
Open: Apr 1 – Oct 31, daily 9 am – 4:45 pm
The Battle of Bergisel on August 13, 1809 under the command of Andreas Hofer is illustrated on 1000 m2 of canvas. It is a unique work of art with lifelike perspective. Aside from depicting an historic battle scene, it offers a good view of old Innsbruck. Artist Michael Zeno Diemer (1867-1939) became world famous with this oil painting.

Excerpt from the Giant Panorama Painting

Stadtarchiv (Innsbruck Municipal Archive)

Badgasse 2
Telephone: 58 73 80
Open: Mondays – Thursdays 8 am – 12 noon and 2 pm – 6 pm, Fridays 8 am – 1 pm
Exhibitions illustrating the history of Innsbruck.

Stiftsmuseum des Prämonstratenser-Chorherren-Stiftes (Premonstratensian Abbey Museum)

Klostergasse 7
Telephone: 58 30 48
Open: only for groups by appointment
The Norberti Room and the adjoining rooms hold a vast collection of sculptures and paintings from the Gothic to the Baroque. Numerous documents, globes, including one by Peter Anich (1758), coin and copperplate collections are on display.

Tiroler Landesmuseum Ferdinandeum (Tyrolean State Museum Ferdinandeum)

Museumstrasse 15
Telephone: 59 4 89
Open: May 1 – Sept 30, daily 10 am – 5 pm; Oct 1 – Apr 30, Tuesdays – Saturdays 10 am - 12 noon and 2 pm – 5 pm, Sundays and public holidays 10 am – 1 pm (closed Jan 1, Nov 1 and Dec 25)

"Apollo Among the Shepards" – by Joseph Anton Koch

As the second oldest regional museum in Austria (the Joanneum in Graz is the oldest), this museum contains works of art, the Tyrolean State Library with its many manuscripts and newspapers, prehistoric and early historic collections, coin and medallion collections, drawings and prints, a collection of Gothic sculptures and paintings, works by Paul Troger, Joseph Anton Koch, Franz von Defregger, Albin Egger Lienz etc., the Old German Gallery (including works by Bernhard Strigel), Dutch Gallery (including works by Rembrandt and Terborch); and the Modern Gallery (20th-century Austrian art including works by Klimt, Schiele and Kokoschka).

Tiroler Landeskundliches Museum – Zeughaus (Tyrolean Regional Museum - Armory)

Zeughausgasse
Telephone: 58 74 39
Open: May 1 – Sept 30, daily 10 am – 5 pm; Oct 1 – Apr 30, Tuesdays – Saturdays 10 am - 12 noon and 2 pm – 5 pm, Sundays and public holidays 10 am – 1 pm (closed Jan 1, Nov 1, and Dec 25)
Emperor Maximilian I's former armory (Zeughaus), displays geological collections of important minerals and fossils, many musical instruments, exhibits on mining as well as metalwork, cartography from the 17th and 18th centuries, hunting and firefighting and the former log drift in the Brandenberg Valley, along with many other exhibits. Another theme highlighted is the history of the Tyrolean militia. Numerous locomotives, carriages, trams and other vehicles are on display on the ground floor and in the courtyard.

★ Tiroler Volkskunstmuseum (Museum of Tyrolean Folk Art)

Universitätsstrasse 2
Telephone: 58 43 02
Open: Mondays – Saturdays 9 am – 5 pm, Sundays and public holidays 9 am – 12 noon (closed Jan. 1, Shrove Tuesday, Easter Sunday, Whit Sunday, Corpus Christi, Nov 1 and Dec 25)
The ground floor contains some 100 nativity crèches dating from

Traditional costumes of the Puster Valley, South Tyrol (first half of the 19th century)

Interior from Dimaro, Trent (second half of the 17th century)

1750 to 1985. On the first floor are six Gothic wood-paneled parlors, models of farmhouses, furniture, household equipment, farm tools, guild memorabilia, carnival masks and costumes. The second floor houses eight wood-paneled parlors from the Renaissance and Baroque, rustic painted and carved furniture from all parts of Tyrol as well as traditional costumes and devotionary objects.

The Museum of Folk Art and the Court Church (Hofkirche) have one entrance. In the Court Church are the (empty) tomb of Emperor Maximilian I, the largest Renaissance tomb in the German-speaking countries with 28 larger-than-life bronze statues (depicting Maximilian's ancestors and relatives), and the graves of the Tyrolean Freedom Fighters Andreas Hofer, Josef Speckbacher and Brother Joachim Haspinger. The church's organ and that of the Silver Chapel (Silberne Kapelle) are renowned.

A visit to the ★ **Alpine Zoo (Alpenzoo)** is lots of fun year-round for young and old alike.

The Innsbruck Alpine Zoo is the only zoo of its kind in all of Europe. Housed in spacious aviaries and cages are a large number of animals that were or still are indigenous to the Alps. Its unique location in beautiful mountain terrain has brought the zoo great esteem and popularity with international zoologists and the general public. It is a discovery, educational, research and nature preservation zoo. Moreover, it has its own Alpine Zoo School, which organizes tours designed especially for kids.

The zoo is also successful in breeding bearded vultures, otters and ibexes. Some animals are donated to other zoos or exchanged for other animals. Furthermore, the zoo also takes part in resettlement projects, i.e. the bearded vulture in the Rauris Valley in Salzburg.

How to get to the Alpine Zoo:

By foot, cross the river on the Innsteg near the Court Garden (Hofgarten) and then follow Weiherburggasse. Otherwise, you can start from the Weiherburgsteg (wooden covered bridge) and follow the well-marked path to the zoo for 20 minutes.

By car, take St. Nikolausgasse and Weiherburggasse (good signs along the way). Parking at the zoo is limited!

Shuttle buses leave from Maria-Theresien-Strasse/Altes Landhaus on the hour 10 am – 5 pm to the zoo and return on the half-hour 10:30 am – 5:30 pm. Shuttle service runs daily between May 15th and Sept. 30th.

Take the funicular (Hungerburgbahn) to the "Alpenzoo" stop and walk approximately 10 minutes to the zoo.

Combined ticket: fare to zoo by **funicular (Hungerburgbahn)** - admission to the zoo - return fare on the funicular.

Alpine Zoo Earth-Friendly Ticket: Public transportation to the valley station of the funicular (Hungerburgbahn) – fare to the "Alpenzoo" station – zoo admission - return fare on the funicular.

Alpenzoo (Alpine Zoo)
Weiherburggasse 37
Telephone: 29 23 23
Fax: 29 30 89
Open: during daylight-saving time daily 9 am – 6 pm; otherwise 9 am – 5 pm

A visit to the **Schmetterlingshaus (Butterfly House)** in the southern part of the Hofgarten is really interesting but very hot! Here you can get a close-up view of exotic, live butterflies.
Schmetterlingshaus
Rennweg 8
Telephone: 58 48 03 27
Open: June – Sept daily 10 am – 5 pm

Kids love to ride in a **horse-drawn carriage** through the inner city. The carriages await their passengers in front of the Tyrolean State Theater on Rennweg.

Playgrounds: in the Court Garden (Hofgarten), Rapoldipark (Pradl), at Gramartboden (near the inn "Gramartboden"), Grünwaldboden (Sadrach), Judenbühel (below the Alpine Zoo) and on the Inn (between the bottom station of the funicular and the Innsteg).

A hike along the **nature trail (Waldlehrpfad)** above Sadrach is very informative.

The University of Innsbruck's **Botanical Garden** with large greenhouses and an aquarium is well worth a visit.
Botanischer Garten (Botanical Garden)
Botanikerstrasse/Sternwartestrasse
Telephone: 507-5910
Open: during daylight-saving time 7:30 am – 7 pm;
otherwise 7:30 am – 4:30 pm;
greenhouses open Thursdays and first Sunday of each month
1 pm – 4 pm

The Court Garden (Hofgarten) – a winter fairy tale come true

Favorite Excursions in and around Innsbruck

1 Take an exciting ride to Hungerburg (868 m) with the funicular for a beautiful view of Innsbruck.

2 Walk from Hungerburg to the Gasthof Gramartboden (inn) and continue north along Nisslsteig (trail) up to the Alpine pasture Höttinger Alm (1,487 m). Walking time: 2 1/2 hours.

Höttinger Alm, a tempting place to linger

3 Hike from Hungerburg past the Gasthof Gramartboden (inn) to the popular pilgrimage church Höttinger Bild (905 m). Walking time: 1 hour.

4 From Hungerburg, take the paths Rosnerweg and Hueberweg to the Gasthaus Rechenhof (inn, 869 m). Continue past Canisiusbründl (inn) to Rum. Walking time: 2 hours. Return by bus to the valley station of the funicular (Hungerburgbahn).

5 Follow the path from Hungerburg over the Alpine pasture Arzler Alm (1,067 m) to Rumer Alm (1,243 m). Walking time: 2 hours.

6 Hike from Hungerburg over the Alpine pastures Rumer Alm, Vintlalm (1,567 m) and Thaurer Alm (1,464 m) and descend to Thaur. Walking time: 4 1/2 hours. Return by bus to the valley station of the funicular (Hungerburgbahn).

7 Take the cable car (Norkettenbahn) from Hungerburg to Seegrube (1,905 m) and continue to Hafelekar (2,269 m), the top station.

8 From the Hafelekar station, take the well laid-out paths Hermann-Buhl-Weg and Goethe-Weg to the Pfeishütte (1,922 m, hut). From there, descend by way of Arzler Scharte and Arzler Reise to return to Hungerburg. Walking time: 5 1/2 hours.

Hermann Buhl was considered the best mountain climber of his generation. He is credited with being the first to climb many of Austria's mountains and in 1953 was the first to make a solo climb of the 8,125-m-high Nanga Parbat in the Himalayas.

9 Ride the funicular (Hungerburgbahn) to the "Alpenzoo" stop and take the almost level path, Schillerweg or Richardsweg, to the Alpine Zoo in approximately 10 minutes. A visit to the zoo is always worth your while and is a treat for young and old alike!

10 From Arzl on the outskirts of Innsbruck, tour the stations of the cross up to Kalvarienberg with its little chapel. Walking time: 45 minutes. Beautiful view of Innsbruck and the surrounding area.

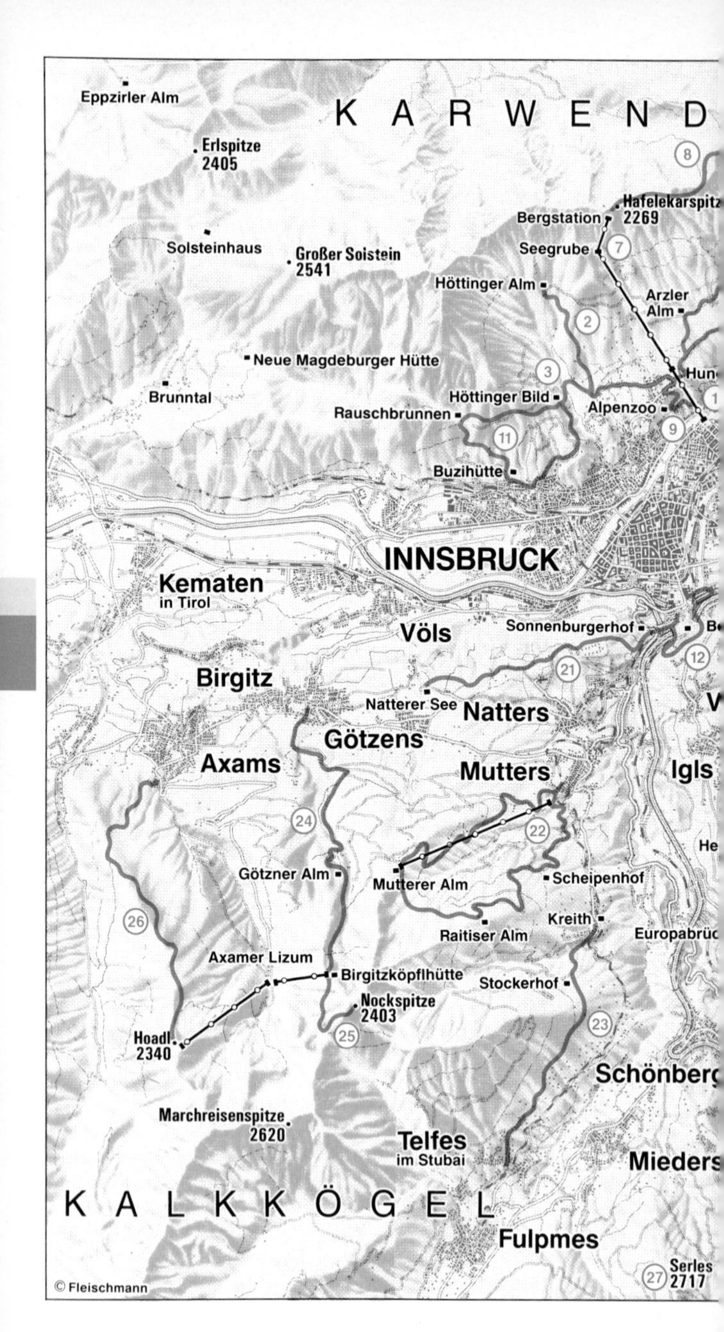
Eppzirler Alm
KARWEND
Erlspitze
2405
Hafelekarspitz
Bergstation
2269
Seegrube
Solsteinhaus
Großer Solstein
2541
Höttinger Alm
Arzler
Alm
Neue Magdeburger Hütte
Brunntal
Höttinger Bild
Rauschbrunnen
Alpenzoo
Buzihütte
INNSBRUCK
Kematen
in Tirol
Völs
Sonnenburgerhof
Birgitz
Natterer See
Natters
Götzens
Axams
Mutters
Igls
Götzner Alm
Mutterer Alm
Scheipenhof
Kreith
Raitiser Alm
Europabrüc
Axamer Lizum
Birgitzköpflhütte
Stockerhof
Nockspitze
2403
Hoadl
2340
Schönberg
Marchreisenspitze
2620
Telfes
im Stubai
Mieders
KALKKÖGEL
Fulpmes
Serles
2717
© Fleischmann

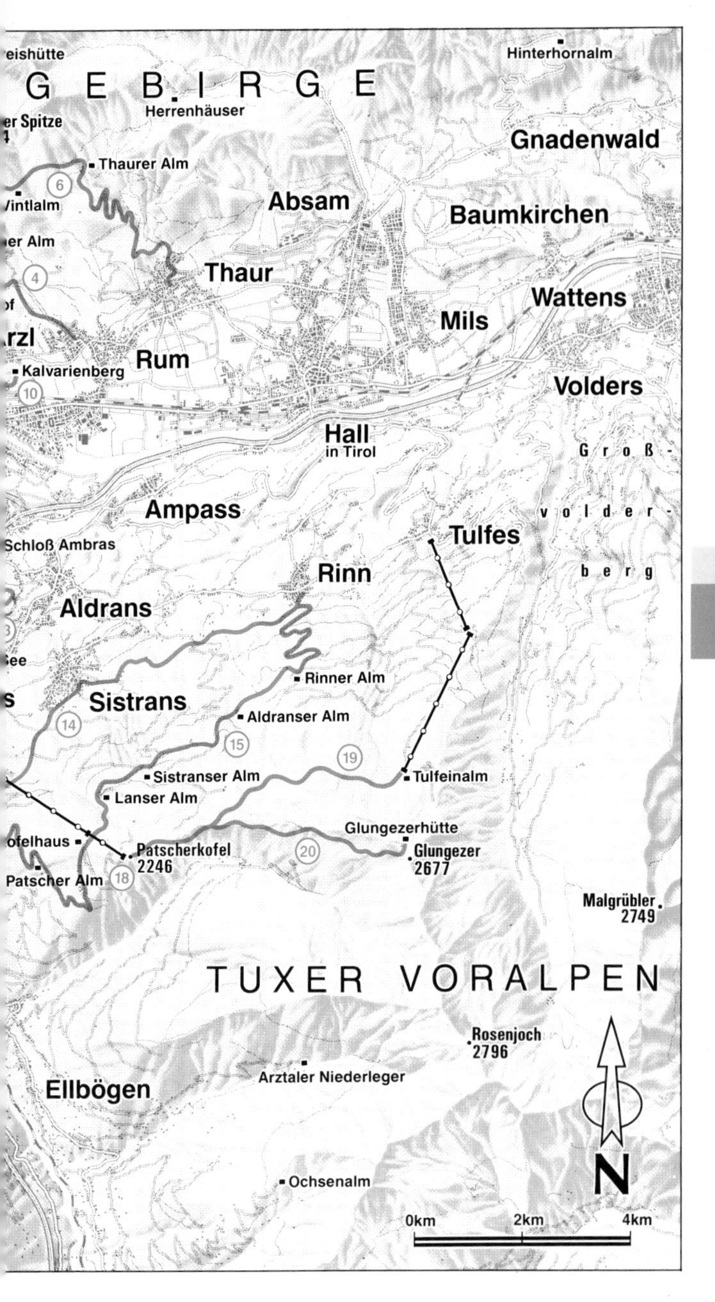
eishütte
Hinterhornalm
G E B I R G E
Herrenhäuser
er Spitze
Gnadenwald
Thaurer Alm
6
Vintlalm
Absam
Baumkirchen
er Alm
4
Thaur
Wattens
Mils
rzl
Rum
Kalvarienberg
10
Volders
Hall
in Tirol
G r o ß -
v o l d e r -
b e r g
Ampass
Tulfes
Schloß Ambras
Rinn
Aldrans
ee
Rinner Alm
Sistrans
Aldranser Alm
14
15
19
Sistranser Alm
Tulfeinalm
Lanser Alm
Glungezerhütte
ofelhaus
Patscherkofel
2246
20
Glungezer
2677
Patscher Alm
18
Malgrübler
2749
TUXER VORALPEN
Rosenjoch
2796
Arztaler Niederleger
Ellbögen
N
Ochsenalm
0km
2km
4km

⑪ From Sadrach in the northwest of Innsbruck, hike past the Buzihütte to Rauschbrunnen (1,088m) for a great view! Continue along Knappensteig (trail) to Höttinger Bild and past the Gasthof Planötzenhof (inn) to return to the starting point. Walking time: 3 hours.

⑫ Take a beautiful stroll through the Sill Gorge (Sillschlucht) around Bergisel. Depart from the Basilica of Wilten. Walking time: 1 1/2 hours.

⑬ Depart from the "Schloss Ambras" stop of the No. 6 tram to Igls and hike past the Jausenstation Vogelhütte (inn) to Mühlsee and Lanser See (lakes). Walking time: 2 hours.

⑭ Walk along Speckbacherweg (trail) from Patsch via Sistrans to Rinn. Walking time: 3 1/2 - 4 hours.

Josef Speckbacher was born in Gnadenwald on July 13, 1767 and married into the Schmiedererhof farm in Rinn in 1794, which he then farmed. In 1809 he took part in the Battle of Bergisel with Andreas Hofer and Brother Joachim Haspinger. He is considered one of Tyrol's foremost patriots. He died in Hall in Tirol on March 28, 1820; his gravestone is in the wall of the Parish Church in Hall. In 1858 his remains were moved to the Court Church (Hofkirche) in Innsbruck, where he now lies beside Andreas Hofer and Brother Joachim Haspinger.

⑮ From Rinn, hike over the Alpine pastures of Rinner Alm (1,394m), Aldranser Alm (1,511m), Sistranser Alm (1,608m) and Lanser Alm (1,718m) up to the Patscherkofelhaus (1,964m, hut). Descend via Patscher Alm (1,694m) to Patsch. Walking time: 6 1/2 hours.

⑯ Depart from the parking lot north of the Gasthaus Grünwalderhof (inn) in Patsch and walk to the popular pilgrimage church Heiligwasser (1,234m). Walking time: 45 minutes.

⑰ Take the cable car Patscherkofel-Bahn from Igls to the Patscherkofelhaus (1,964 m, hut).

⑱ Hike from the Patscherkofelhaus up to Patscherkofel (2,264m).

*The **Men's downhill** skiing events of the Winter Olympics took place on the northern slopes of Patscherkofel. The winners follow:*

1964: 1. Egon Zimmermann (A)
2. Leo Lacroix (F)
3. Wolfgang Bartels (D)
1976: 1. Franz Klammer (A)
2. Bernhard Russi (CH)
3. Herbert Plank (I)

Walking time: 1 hour, or travel by chairlift.

⑲ Walk from the Patscherkofelhaus (hut) along Zirbenweg (trail), which is beautiful in June with Alpine rose blossoms, past the Jausenstation Boscheben (2,035m, inn) to the Alpine pasture Tulfeinalm (2,035m). Walking time: 3 hours. From there, ride the chairlift down to Tulfes and take the bus back to Igls or Innsbruck.

⑳ Depart from the Patscherkofelhaus to the Jausenstation Boscheben (2,035 m, inn) and on to the Glungezerhütte (2,600 m, hut). Walking time: 4 hours.

㉑ From the "Sonnenburgerhof" stop on the Stubai Tram (Stubaitalbahn) hike over Natterer Boden and Eichhof to Natterer See (lake). Walking time: 2 1/2 hours.

22 From Mutters go past the Nockhof (1,264 m), to the Gasthof Mutterer Alm (1,608 m, inn). Continue across the Alpine pasture Raitiser Alm (1,553 m) and past Scheipenhof (1,139 m) back to the starting point. Walking time: 5 hours.

23 From the "Kreith" stop on the Stubai Tram (Stubaitalbahn), hike past Stockerhof (1,156 m) and across Telfeser Wiesen (beautiful larch-lined meadows) to Telfes in the Stubai Valley. Walking time: 2 1/2 hours. Return to the starting point or to Innsbruck with the Stubai Tram.

24 From Götzens, hike over the Alpine pasture Götzner Alm (1,542m) to the Birgitzköpflhütte (2,035m, hut). Walking time: 4 hours.

25 Take the lift at "Axamer Lizum" to the Birgitzköpflhütte (2,035m, hut) and hike from there to the Nockspitze (2,403m). Walking time: 1 1/2 hours.

26 Take the bus from Axams to Axamer Lizum and then the funicular to Hoadl (2,340m). Magnificent view! Return to the starting point by way of the Kögelesteig and Brunnensteig trails. Walking time: 2 hours.

27 Hike from the pilgrimage chapel Maria Waldrast up the Serles (2,717 m). Walking time: 3 hours. It's a once-in-a-lifetime experience to be on a mountain peak at sunrise!

Several skiing events were held at Axamer Lizum during the Winter Olympics in 1964 and 1976 with the following medalists:

Women's Downhill

1964:		1976:	
	1. Christl Haas (A)		*1. Rosi Mittermaier (D)*
	2. Edith Zimmermann (A)		*2. Brigitte Totschnig (A)*
	3. Traudl Hecher (A)		*3. Cynthia Nelson (USA)*

Women's Slalom

1964:		1976:	
	1. Christine Goitschel (F)		*1. Rosi Mittermaier (D)*
	2. Marielle Goitschel (F)		*2. Claudia Giordani (I)*
	3. Jean Marlene Saubert (USA)		*3. Hanni Wenzel (LIE)*

Women's Giant Slalom

1964:		1976:	
	1. Marielle Goitschel (F)		*1. Kathy Kreiner (CAN)*
	2. Christine Goitschel (F)		*2. Rosi Mittermaier (D)*
	3. Jean Marlene Saubert (USA)		*3. Daniele Debernard (F)*

Men's Slalom

1964:		1976:	
	1. Josef Stiegler (A)		*1. Piero Gros (I)*
	2. William Winston Kidd (USA)		*2. Gustav Thöni (I)*
	3. James Frederic Heuga (USA)		*3. Willy Frommelt (LIE)*

Men's Giant Slalom

1964:		1976:	
	1. Francois Bonlieu (F)		*1. Heini Hemmi (CH)*
	2. Karl Schranz (A)		*2. Ernst Good (CH)*
	3. Josef Stiegler (A)		*3. Ingemar Stenmark (SWE)*

→ Another great excursion destination, but one that is more easily accessible by car on the Brenner Autobahn (toll), is the Europe Bridge (Europabrücke), the tallest bridge in Europe. At a height of 190 m it spans the Wipp Valley for a length of 777 m. The bridge has been open since 1963. The Europe Chapel (Europakapelle), built by Architect Hubert Prachensky in 1963 at the south end of the bridge, was decorated with frescoes by the artist Karl Plattner of Bolzano.

For hikes and Alpine tours in the Innsbruck area we recommend:
KOMPASS Hiking Maps No. 36 "Innsbruck-Brenner" (1:50,000) and No. 036 "Innsbruck und Umgebung" (1:30,000).

Arzler Alm, a hiker's paradise

Important Information – Tips

Telephone area code for Innsbruck from inside Austria: 0512.
Postal Code: A-6020 Innsbruck.

INFORMATION

Tourismusverband Innsbruck-Igls (Innsbruck-Igls Tourist Office)
Burggraben 3
Telephone: 59 8 500
Fax: 59 8 507
Open: Mondays – Fridays 8 am – 6 pm, Saturdays 8 am – 12 noon

Igls Office
Hilberstrasse 15
Telephone: 37 71 01, Fax: 37 89 65
Open: Mondays – Fridays 8:30 am – 12 noon and 2 pm to 6 pm, Saturdays 9 am – 12 noon (only in season)

Innsbruck-Information und Innsbrucker Zimmernachweis (Innsbruck Information and Innsbruck Hotel Information)
Burggraben 3
Telephone: 53 56, Fax: 53 56-43
Open: Mondays – Saturdays 8 am – 7 pm, Sundays and holidays 9 am – 6 pm

This is where to get all important information on Innsbruck.
This is where to change money and buy tickets for events in and around Innsbruck.
This is where to find advance sales for (cheaper!) tickets for public transportation in Innsbruck.

Branch Offices
Office at Main Railroad Station
Telephone: 58 37 66
Open: Apr – Oct daily 9 am – 10 pm, Nov – Mar daily 9 am – 9 pm

West Office at Autobahn Exit
Telephone: 57 35 43
Open: Apr – Oct daily 10 am – 8 pm, Nov – Mar daily 12 noon – 7 pm

East Office at Autobahn Exit
Telephone: 34 64 74
Open: Apr – Oct daily 10 am – 8 pm, Nov – Mar daily 12 noon – 7 pm

South Office on Brennerbundesstrasse
Telephone: 57 79 33
Open: Apr – Oct daily 10 am – 8 pm, Nov – Mar daily 12 noon – 7 pm

North Office on Kranebitter Allee
Telephone: 28 49 91
Open: Mid June – end of Sept daily 10 am – 8 pm

Tirol Info (Tyrol Information)
Bozner Platz 6, 1996 move to Maria-Theresien-Strasse
Telephone: 53 200
Fax: 53 20 150
Open: Mondays – Fridays 8:30 am – 6 pm, Saturdays 9 am – 12 noon

Österreichisches Verkehrsbüro (Austrian National Travel Agency)
Wilhelm-Greil-Strasse 14
Telephone: 57 18 81
Open: Mondays – Fridays 8:30 am – 5:30 pm

ACCOMMODATIONS

Innsbruck and Igls offer a total of approx. 9,000 beds in **hotels, inns, pensions, holiday apartments** and **private homes.** Since there is not enough space to list them all here, please consult one of the above addresses for further information.

> ***Club Innsbruck Card:*** *Anyone who stays in Innsbruck or Igls for at least three nights automatically becomes a member of Club Innsbruck. Members are entitled to participate free of charge in Alpine hiking programs, use the ski and cross-country shuttle buses free of charge and receive discounts on ski passes and cable cars, admission to museums and the Alpine Zoo and at the Tennis Parkclub in Igls. Inquire at your lodgings for the Club Innsbruck Card.*

Youth Hostels

Reservations for groups required.

Österreichischer Jugendherbergsverband (Austrian Youth Hostel Association): Südtiroler Platz 14-16, Telephone: 59 7 77,
Fax: 59 7 77 550

Österreichisches Jugendherbergswerk (Austrian Youth Hostels Federation): Reichenauer Strasse 147,
Telephone: 34 61 79 or 34 61 80
Fax: 34 61 79 12

Reichenauer Strasse 147,
Telephone: 34 61 79 or 34 61 80
Fax: 34 61 79 12; open all year
Innstrasse 95,
Telephone: 28 65 15,
Fax: 28 65 15-14; open all year
Rennweg 17b (Schwedenhaus),
Telephone: 58 58 14; open July - Aug
Radetzkystrasse 47, Telephone: 46 66 82; open all year (closed for two weeks in July)
Sillgasse 8a (MK),
Telephone: 57 13 11;
open in summer
Reichenauer Strasse 68 (youth home of St. Paul's Parish), Telephone: 34 42 91; open in summer

Campgrounds

Kranebitter Allee 214,
Telephone: 28 41 80
Open Apr – Oct

FOR EMERGENCIES

Fire Department	Tel. 122
Police	Tel. 133
Ambulance/ Rescue Helicopter	Tel. 144

Allgemeines öffentliches Landeskrankenhaus (Public Hospital)
(University Clinics) with emergency room: Anichstrasse 35, Telephone: 504 0, Fax: 504 2017

Pharmacies: The approx. 25 pharmacies throughout the city are open Mondays – Fridays 8 am – 12 noon and 2:30 pm – 6 pm, Saturdays 8 am – 12 noon. Pharmacies open at night, on weekends and holidays are posted at every closed pharmacy.

Ärztlicher Funkbereitschaftsdienst (Emergency Medical Service) on weekends and holidays: Sillufer 3, Telephone: 36 00 06
Bundespolizeidirektion und **Fundamt (Police Headquarters** and **Lost and Found):** Kaiserjägerstrasse 8,
Telephone: 59 00
Dr. Pierer Tagesklinik (Dr. Pierer Day Clinic): Leopoldstrasse 1,
Telephone: 59 09, Fax: 59 09 60
Rettung Innsbruck (ambulance service) - Innsbruck City Office of the Austrian Red Cross: Sillufer 3, Telephone: 33 4 44
Sanatorium der Barmherzigen Schwestern (Sanatorium of the Sisters of Mercy): Sennstrasse 1, Telephone: 59 38
Tyrolean Air Ambulance:
Telephone: 22 4 22

SIGHTSEEING (WALKS AND DRIVES)

Information and reservations at Innsbruck-Information:
Burggraben 3:
Telephone: 53 56, Fax: 53 56 43

Licensed tour guides can be hired for **sightseeing tours.**

Large Sightseeing Tour:
By coach including walk through the Old City, approx. 2 hours. Leaves daily at 12 noon from the Main Railroad Station (Hotel Information); additional tours given in summer.

Small Sightseeing Tour:
approx. 1 hour.
Leaves: opposite the Court Church (Hofkirche) at 10:15 am, 12 noon, 2 pm and 3:15 pm from mid May – end of Oct

Nostalgia Sightseeing Tram:
approx. 3 hours.
Runs every Thursday from July - Sept. between Innsbruck and Igls, including city sightseeing.

Horse-Drawn Coaches:
Fiakers wait on Rennweg in front of the State Theater (Landestheater).

A favorite photo op: St. Anne's Column on Maria-Theresien-Strasse

PerPedes is an organization that takes you to the most interesting and most famous attractions in Innsbruck.
Contact: PerPedes Tirol, Culture Sightseeing and Culture Service, Innrain 9/II/10,
Telephone + Fax: 58 36 57

TRAFFIC

Car

Automobile **breakdown service** is available 24 hours a day from
ARBÖ Telephone: 123
ÖAMTC Telephone: 120

ARBÖ Headquarters:
Stadlweg 7
Telephone: 34 51 23
ÖAMTC Headquarters:
Andechsstrasse 81
Telephone: 33 20, Fax: 39 16 12

Car Rental/Car Hire
Ajax: Amraser Strasse 6,
Telephone: 58 32 32
ARAC: Amraser Strasse 84,
Telephone: 34 31 61, Fax: 39 39 57
Avis: Salurner Strasse 15,
Telephone 57 17 54
Buchbinder: Burgenlandstrasse 8,
Telephone: 34 85 65
Europcar Interent:
Salurner Strasse 8,
Telephone: 58 20 60, Fax 58 21 07
Airport Office:
Telephone: 28 56 08
Rent a car: Michael-Gaismair-Strasse 5-7,
Telephone 58 84 68, Fax: 58 45 80
Rolls Royce: Pechestrasse 10,
Telephone: 57 32 00 or
0663 05 91 00
Stolz: Fürstenweg 11/2,
Telephone: 29 12 79 or
0663 85 54 11

Train

Innsbruck's Main Railroad Station is located at the junction of international north-south and east-west rail lines. Other train stations in town: Westbahnhof (Arlberg Line) and Höttinger Bahnhof (Karwendel/Mittenwald Line serving Seefeld).

Hauptbahnhof (Main Railroad Station): Südtiroler Platz,
Telephone: 503 0
Austrian Federal Railways, Innsbruck Headquarters:
Claudiastrasse 2,
Telephone: 503, Fax 503 50 05

Autoreisezug (car train): (reservations: 7:30 am – 7 pm),
Telephone: 503 54 84
Bahn Totalservice (7:30 am – 7 pm), Telephone: 17 00
Rent a Bike: Telephone: 503 53 95
Lost and Found:
Telephone: 503 53 57
Travel Agency at the Railroad Station: Telephone: 503 50 00
Baggage Consignment (Mondays - Saturdays 6:30 am – 11 pm, Sundays 6:30 am – 9:30 pm),
Telephone: 503 53 95
Train information to Munich and beyond (tape-recorded),
Telephone: 15 92
Train information to Vienna, Graz and Villach (tape-recorded),
Telephone: 15 93
Train information to Brenner and beyond (tape-recorded),
Telephone: 15 94
Train information to Bregenz, Buchs and beyond (tape-recorded), Telephone: 15 95
Train information (schedules, ticket prices, Austrian Federal Railways (ÖBB) bus service):
Telephone 17 17

Plane

Innsbruck Airport:
Fürstenweg 180,
Telephone: 22 5 25, Fax: 29 25 40

The airport is served by city bus line "F" leaving from the Main Railroad Station.
Daily and weekly scheduled flights to Amsterdam, Frankfurt, Graz, Linz, Paris, Salzburg, Vienna, Zürich.

Aircraft Services/Panorama Flights
Flugdienst Innsbruck: Fürstenweg 180, Telephone: 22 5 25-390
Heli Trans: Fischerhäuslweg 16, Telephone: 27 85 58, Fax: 27 85 57
Steiger Panorama-Hubschrauber-Rundflüge (helicopter panorama sightseeing), Silberweg 5, Telephone: 29 52 00

Airlines:
Austrian Airlines & Swissair: Adamgasse 7a,
Telephone: 58 29 85, Fax: 57 28 48
Tyrolean Airways:
Fürstenweg 180, Telephone: 22 22

Parking

The entire inner city and many streets in other parts of Innsbruck are **short-term pay-parking zones.** Depending on the zone, parking is limited to 1 1/2 to 3 hours and a fee of 5 or 10 schillings is charged per half hour. Short-term pay-parking zones are in effect from Mondays to Fridays between 9 am and 7 pm and on Saturdays from 9 am to 1 pm (except holidays). Pay at one of the many sidewalk machines and put the slip inside your windshield.

Pay Car Parks (indoors)
Parking fee per hour commenced: ATS 22.

Hotel Maria Theresia, Erlerstrasse, daily 24 hours

Sparkassen-Garage, Sparkassenplatz 1, Mondays – Fridays 7 am – 8 pm, Saturdays 8 am – 1 pm

Tourist Center (Hotel Scandic Crown), Salurner Strasse 15, daily 7 am – 10 pm

Markthalle, Herzog-Sigmund-Ufer 5, Mondays – Fridays 6:30 am – 8 pm, Saturdays 6:30 am – 6 pm, closed holidays

Meinhard-Garage, Meinhardstrasse 5, Mondays - Fridays 7 am – 8 pm (cashier on duty to 7 pm, then pay by machine), Saturdays 8 am – 1 pm, closed holidays

Tiroler Gebietskrankenkasse, Klara-Pölt-Weg 2, Mondays – Fridays 7 am – 7 pm

Landhausplatz, Wilhelm-Greil-Strasse, daily 7 am – 1 am

Hentschelhof, Innrain 25, Mondays – Saturdays 6:30 am – 8 pm

Altstadtgarage, Innrain 4, Mondays – Saturdays 7 am – 1 am (cashier on duty to 10 pm, then pay by machine), Sundays and holidays no cashier on duty

Sillpark-Einkaufspark, Museumstrasse 38, Mondays – Thursdays 8:30 am – 8 pm, Fridays 8:30 am – 9 pm, Saturdays 8:30 am – 2 pm

Pay Parking (outdoors)

Pay parking is currently available for cars and buses on the site of the former Fennerkaserne, entrance from Kaiserjägerstrasse. From there it is only a few minutes' walk through the Court Garden (Hofgarten) to the heart of town.

Park + Ride (P + R)

This parking area is located at the Ice Stadium (Eisstadion) and is open daily from 7 am – 7 pm (vehicles may leave later). The parking fee is ATS 30 per day and includes a one-day ticket for the Innsbruck Public Transit Service (IVB). Parking is free of charge for holders of IVB (public transit) passes good for min. one week. The bus line "P+R" runs from this parking area to the inner city every ten minutes from 6:50 am - 9 am and from 4:05 pm – 6:55 pm Mondays to Fridays and from 6:50 am – 9 am and from 11:55 am – 1:05 pm on Saturdays. In the off hours the other IVB lines can be used; the bus stop for the "K" and "J" lines is nearby. The "P+R" bus stops at the entrance to the Tivoli soccer stadium, on Kaiserschützenplatz, at the Arch of Triumph, on Maria-Theresien-Strasse, at the Tiroler Landesmuseum Ferdinandeum and on Anton-Eder-Strasse.

Public Transportation

When traveling in town and the surroundings please use public transportation and leave your car home.
Single tickets can be purchased from the driver. One-day passes, four-trip tickets and one-week passes are available on an advance-sale basis.

Advance Ticket Sales

City office of the Innsbruck Public Transit Service (IVB):
Museumstrasse 23,
Telephone 5307 102, Fax: 5307 192
Open Mondays - Fridays 7:30 am – 6 pm
Customer Sales Office of Verkehrsverbund Tirol (VVT):
Eduard-Bodem-Gasse 8,
Telephone: 36 59 20. Open Mondays – Thursdays 7:30 am – 12 noon and 1 pm – 5 pm, Fridays 7:30 am – 11:30 am.
In numerous tobacco shops in the city.
At Innsbruck-Information, Burggraben 3.

Tram and Bus Lines

Public transportation runs from approx. 6 am to approx. 11 pm. Schedules are posted at the bus/tram stops.

Tram line 1: Saggen – Bergisel

Tram line 3: Amras – city center

Tram line 6: Saggen – Igls

Tram line Stb: Innsbruck – Stubai Valley

Bus line A: Main Railroad Station – Hötting

Bus line B: Pradl – Höttinger Au

Bus line C: Sieglanger/Mentlberg - Rum/Sanatorium

Bus line D/E: "Dörferlinie" to outlying villages

Bus line F: Main Railroad Station – Airport

Bus line H: Hörtnaglsiedlung (does not run on Sundays)

Bus line J: Main Railroad Station – Igls

Bus line K: Amras – St. Nikolaus

Bus line LK: Bozner Platz – Kranebitten

Bus line N: Bozner Platz – Hungerburg

Bus line O: Olympic Village – Allerheiligen

Bus line P+R: Park + Ride parking area at Ice Stadium to city center; see p. 74.

Bus line R: Main Railroad Station - Reichenau

Bus line RR: Youth Hostel/Reichenauer Strasse – Archenweg (does not run Saturdays or Sundays)

Bus line S: Main Railroad Station via autobahn – Hall in Tirol – Mils (runs only workdays)

Bus line 4: Main Railroad Station - Hall in Tirol

Buses operated by the Austrian government (Bundesbusse) and by **private companies,** which serve all parts of Tyrol, leave from the bus depot south of the Main Railroad Station.

Taxis

Telephone: 53 11, 35 5 00 or 17 18

Special Public Transit Tickets

Abenderlebnis Seegrube (Seegrube Evening Adventure): Every Thursday evening, cable car to Seegrube, 6 pm - 11 pm

Ticket Alpenzoo-Umweltkarte (Alpine Zoo Environmental Ticket): Special "souvenir postcard" ticket good for public transportation to and from the zoo plus zoo admission for one person. Obtainable from Innsbruck-Information, Burggraben 3.

Bergwanderkarte (Mountain Hiking Ticket): This ticket is valid from the date of its first use for three consecutive days on the Hungerburg Funicular, Nordkette Cable Car and Patscherkofel Cable Car. Obtainable at the cashier of all three cable cars or from Innsbruck-Information, Burggraben 3.

Besucherkarte Innsbruck-Igls (Innsbruck-Igls Visitors Card): This ticket entitles the holder to admission to various museums as well as one free day on the Innsbruck public transit facilities and one round-trip on the Patscherkofel Cable Car or the Nordkette Cable Car to Seegrube.

Zirben Trail Round-Trip Ticket (Zirbenweg-Rundtour-Karte): Special for hiking enthusiasts! This ticket is good for a one-way ride each on the Patscherkofel Cable Car in Igls, the Glungezer Cable Car in Tulfes and the bus (Bundesbus) between Igls and Tulfes, in either direction. Obtainable at the cashier of either cable car.

Shuttle Service

To the Alpine Zoo: from May 15 – Sept 30 daily from 10 am to 5 pm. Departures on the hour from Maria-Theresien-Strasse (Altes Landhaus) and on the half hour from the Alpine Zoo.

Cable Cars in and Around Innsbruck

Axams
Axamer Lizum Cable Cars:
Telephone: (52 34) 82 40

Igls
Patscherkofel Cable Car: Bilgeristrasse 18, Telephone: 37 72 34

Innsbruck
Hungerburg Funicular: Rennweg 41, Telephone 29 22 50 or 58 61 58
From the "Alpenzoo" station it is a ten-minute walk to the Alpine Zoo.

Nordkette Cable Car:
Höhenstrasse 15,
Telephone: 29 33 44

Mutters
Muttereralm Cable Car:
Nockhofweg 39,
Telephone: 54 82 80

Start your hike with the Nordkette Cable Car

Oberperfuss
Rangger Köpfl Cable Cars:
Telephone: (05232) 81 3 47

Tulfes:
Glungezer Cable Car:
Telephone: (05223) 83 21

CULTURE – ENTERTAINMENT – RELAXATION – TYROLEAN CRAFTSMEN

Tyrolean Evening

Performances are given at the Gasthof Sandwirt am Inn, Reichenauer Strasse 151, the Messe-Saal (trade fair hall), Ing. Etzel-Strasse, and the Gasthof Sailer, Adamgasse 8.
For reservations and information contact the organizers: Geschwister Gundolf, Aurain 1, A-6063 Rum, Telephone: 26 34 97 or 26 32 63, Fax: 26 83 38

Dining

It would be difficult and take too much space to list all of

Antique signs point the way to friendly old inns

nnsbruck's coffeehouses, restaurants and inns. But this much can be said here at any rate: Innsbruck is home to many well-run restaurants offering traditional Tyrolean and Austrian fare as well as international specialties.

The following is a short **selection** of the city's better known hotels and restaurants:

Engl: Innstrasse 22, Telephone: 28 31 12
Europa Tyrol: Südtiroler Platz 2, Telephone: 59 31
Europastüberl: Brixner Strasse 6, Telephone: 59 31
Goldener Adler: Herzog-Friedrich-Strasse 6, Telephone: 58 63 34
Goldener Hirsch: Seilergasse 9, Telephone: 58 13 40
Grauer Bär: Universitätsstrasse 7, Telephone: 59 24
Sailer: Adamgasse 8, Telephone: 53 63
Schwarzer Adler: Kaiserjägerstrasse 2, Telephone: 58 71 09
Tiroler Weinstube: Gumpp-strasse 38, Telephone: 34 32 03
Weinhaus Happ: Herzog-Friedrich-Strasse 14, Telephone: 58 29 80
Weisses Kreuz: Herzog-Friedrich-Strasse 31, Telephone: 59 4 79
Weisses Rössl: Kiebachgasse 8, Telephone: 58 30 57
Wilder Mann: Museumstrasse 28, Telephone: 58 32 95

Try your hand at 44 original Austrian recipes available in ***"Austrian Specialties,"*** *KOMPASS Kitchen Delights, No. 1718, published by Verlag Fleischmann & Mair GmbH.*

Bars - Dancing - Discos

American Bar: Maria-Theresien-Strasse 10, Telephone: 58 67 60
Clima Nightclub: Zeughausgasse 7, Telephone 58 15 40
Club Filou: Stiftgasse, Telephone: 58 02 56
Nightclub Innsbruck Lady O: Brunecker Strasse 2a, Telephone: 58 64 32
Queen-Ann Dancing: Amraser Strasse 6, Telephone: 57 51 55

Theaters

Alt-Innsbrucker Bauerntheater und Ritterspiele at the Kulturgasthaus Bierstindl: Klostergasse 6, Telephone: 57 21 00

Innsbrucker Keller Theater (cellar theater): Adolf-Pichler-Platz 8, Telephone: 58 07 43 or 57 75 90

Kammerspiele: Universitätsstrasse, telephone and advance ticket sales see Tyrolean State Theater

Tiroler Landesjugendtheater und Märchenbühne (for young people and children): Messegelände, Ing.-Etzel-Strasse 31, Telephone: 57 53 62 or 20 58 68

Tiroler Landestheater (Tyrolean State Theater): opera, operetta, musical, drama, comedy, ballet; Rennweg 2, Telephone: 52 0 74, reservations and advance ticket sales: Telephone: 52 0 74 4, Fax: 52 0 74 333

Tiroler Volksbühne Blaas (Breinössl-Bühne): Maria-Theresien-Strasse 12, Telephone: 58 60 01. Same-day box office from 7 pm, Telephone: 58 59 02

Cultural Centers

Treibhaus: Angerzellgasse 8,
Telephone: 58 68 74
Utopia: Tschamlerstrasse 8,
Telephone: 58 85 87, Fax: 56 34 27

Art Galleries

Galerie im Andechshof: Innrain 1,
Telephone: 57 26 32
Galerie im Taxis-Palais: Maria-Theresien-Strasse 45,
Telephone: 58 93 22
Galerie Thoman: Adamgasse 7a,
Telephone: 57 57 85
Galerie Thomas Flora: Herzog-Friedrich-Strasse 5,
Telephone: 57 74 02
Stadtturmgalerie: Herzog-Friedrich-Strasse 21,
Telephone: 57 81 54
Theresien-Galerie: Maria-Theresien-Strasse 10,
Telephone: 58 10 17
Tiroler Kunstpavillon: Rennweg 8a,
Telephone: 58 11 33, Fax: 58 59 71

Exhibitions

Stadtarchiv (Municipal Archive): exhibitions on the history of Innsbruck, Badgasse 2,
Telephone: 58 73 80
Tiroler Handelskammer (Tyrolean Chamber of Commerce): Meinhardstrasse 12,
Telephone: 53 10
Tiroler Landeskundliches Museum - Zeughaus, Zeughausgasse, Telephone: 58 74 39
Tiroler Landesmuseum Ferdinandeum: Museumstrasse 15,
Telephone: 59 4 89

Fairs

At the Fair Grounds (Messegelände): Falkstrasse 2-4,
Telephone: 58 59 11, Fax: 58 42 90
or at Congress Innsbruck:
Rennweg 3,
Telephone 59 36, Fax: 59 36 7

A sampling of Innsbruck's fairs:
FAFGA Trade Fair for Tourism and Gastronomy
Innsbruck Spring Fair
(Building – Home Furnishings – Garden – Leisure)
Innsbruck Autumn Fair
Senior-Aktuell
Studien- und Berufsinformationsmesse
Tyrolean Art and Antiques Fair
Tyrolean Handcrafts and Souvenir Fair
Tiroler Trödel Tage

Concerts

Church and organ concerts are frequently held in the Jesuit Church, the Court Church and the Silver Chapel, in Wilten Basilica and in the Igls Parish Church.
Concerts by Tyrolean brass bands, foreign bands and choral groups are given at the Golden Roof, at Congress Innsbruck and in the Court Garden.
Concerts are often held in the Hofgartencafé.
The **Festival Weeks of Early Music (Festwochen der Alten Musik)** were inaugurated in 1977 and aim to revive the former glory of Innsbruck's court music. The concerts, that are meanwhile world famed, are given on ancient instruments and feature Baroque operas. The festival is held each August at the State Theater, Spanish Hall of Ambras Castle, Wilten Abbey Church and the Giants' Room of the Court Palace. For

information and reservations, contact Innsbruck-Information: Burggraben 3, Telephone: 53 56.

During the summer, the **Ambras Castle Concerts (Ambraser Schlosskonzerte)** are given in the Spanish Hall of Ambras Castle. For information and reservations, contact Innsbruck-Information: Burggraben 3, Telephone: 53 56, or the organizer "Verein Ambraser Schlosskonzerte":

Schöpfstrasse 20,

Telephone: 57 10 32, Fax: 56 31 42.

Congress Innsbruck

Rennweg 3,

Telephone: 59 36, Fax: 59 36 7

"No congress too big, no congress too small." Numerous events are held in Innsbruck under this motto all year long. For example, balls, exhibitions, meetings, congresses and symposiums.

Cinemas

Central Kino: Maria-Theresien-Strasse 17-19,
Telephone: 58 80 78

Cine-Royal: Innrain 16,
Telephone: 58 63 85

Cinematograph: Museumstrasse 31, Telephone: 57 85 00

Cineplexx: Wilhelm-Greil-Strasse 23, Telephone: 58 14 57

Leo-Lichtspiele: Anichstrasse 36,
Telephone: 58 63 08

Metropol-Lichtspiele; Innstrasse 5,
Telephone: 28 33 10

Olympia Kino: Höttinger Au 24a,
Telephone: 28 35 62

Casino

Salurner Strasse 15
Telephone: 58 70 40,
Fax: 58 70 40 66

Libraries

AEP-Frauenbibliothek (AEP Women's Library):
Leopoldstrasse 31a,
Telephone: 58 36 98
Bücherei der Kammer für Arbeiter und Angestellte für Tirol: Maximilianstrasse 7,
Telephone: 53 40 312
Bücherei für Landesbedienstete:
Maria-Theresien-Strasse 42,
Telephone: 58 29 92
Büchereistelle des Bundes für Erwachsenenbildung für Tirol,
Hofburg, Rennweg 1,
Telephone: 57 37 05
Landesjugendbücherei Taxis-Palais: Maria-Theresien-Strasse 45,
Telephone: 508 571
Stadtbücherei Innsbruck (Municipal Library): Burggraben 3,
Telephone: 53 60 499
Tiroler Landesmuseum Ferdinandeum: Museumstrasse 15,
Telephone: 59 4 89
Universitäts-Bibliothek (University Library): Innrain 50,
Telephone: 5070

Events Throughout the Year

For further information, contact Innsbruck-Information: Burggraben 3,
Telephone: 53 56

January

New Year's Eve/New Year's Day: fireworks illuminate the city skyline at midnight
New Year's Concert

Intersport Ski Jumping Tournament at Bergisel
Epiphany Carols sung in the city and countryside by boys and girls of the Catholic Youth Organization dressed as the Three Magi. They wander from house to house requesting donations for projects in the Third World.

February

"Mullerlaufen," an ancient carnival tradition (Igls, Rum, Thaur).
On mardi gras, the day before Ash Wednesday, the city is populated by costumed carnival-goers, while carnival floats travel the streets.

March/April

Lenten crèches portraying Christ's passion are on display in many churches (Thaur, Zirl, Götzens).
Palm Sunday: processions with decorated pussy willow and the Palm Sunday donkey (Thaur, Hall).
As of Good Friday, many churches show the Holy Sepulcher.
Easter Sunday: Easter bonfires are set and food is blessed.

May/June

Maypoles are erected on May 1.
Corpus Christi processions
Mountain bonfires on the Feast of the Sacred Heart
Mountain bonfires at midsummer

June-August

Ambras Castle Concerts (see Concerts)

August

Festival Weeks of Early Music (see Concerts)

November

Lantern-light children's procession to celebrate St. Martin's Day, about Nov. 11

December

St. Nicholas Procession on December 5
Tyrolean Advent Carolling
Nativity plays
Christmas season: crèches are visited in churches and private homes (Thaur, Götzens, Axams, Zirl).

Markets

Farmers Market: in the market hall, Herzog-Sigmund-Ufer, Mondays – Saturdays 7 am – 1 pm
Christmas Market (Christkindlmarkt): in the Old City; from the last Saturday in November to Dec. 22.
Flea Market: Every 1st and 3rd Saturday morning in the courtyard of the New City Hall
Hubertus Market: At the entrance to the market hall, last week of October to mid November
Second-Hand Market (Trödelmarkt): Every Saturday morning on Innrain, near Johanneskirche (St. John's Church)

Shopping

Innsbruck's city center offers approx. 250 shops. Department stores and malls with ample parking are located on the city's outskirts. Shops are generally open Mondays – Fridays 8:30 am – 6 pm (only few shops are closed at lunch time) and Saturdays 8 am – 12 noon. On the first Saturday of each month shops can stay open until 5 pm. Don't forget to look for shops announcing "tax-free for tourists." This means that on purchases over ATS 1,000 the 20% VAT is refunded at the border. Ask the shop to give you the Tax Refund Cheque. Many shops in town offer the Innsbruck Service Card with a minimum purchase of ATS 500. This card entitles you to an ATS 10 discount in park garages or, if you present it to a bus driver, one ticket for the Innsbruck Public Transit System.

Watch Tyrolean Craftsmen at Their Work

Special workshop for **wind instruments:** Since 1875. Musikhaus Rudolf Tutz, Innstrasse 51, Telephone: 28 63 30, Fax: 29 54 62

Master Violin Maker:
Wolfgang Kozák, Universitätsstrasse 3/1, Telephone: 57 34 02, Mondays, Wednesdays and Fridays 7:30 am – 6 pm, Saturdays 7:30 am – 11:45 am

Violin Maker: Violin making in the Italian tradition, old and new instruments, bows, consultation, specialist in restoration and Baroque instruments, maker of gambas, newest specialization: electric pick-up and solid-body violins. Bernhard Costa, Museumstrasse 19, Telephone: 56 19 08, Mondays – Fridays 10 am – 12 noon and 3 pm – 6 pm (closed Wednesday afternoons)

Wooden Toys: Manufacture of limited numbers of hand-made children's toys, rocking horses etc. Only local woods used. All products vegetable oil-impregnated. Klaus Mader, Viaduktbogen 148, Telephone: 57 03 06, Mondays – Fridays: 3 pm – 6 pm

Glas-Blowing Workshop:
Günter Brandt, Pradler Strasse 23, Telephone: 39 12 96

Glass from the Master:
Engraving. Herbert Aigner, Amraser Strasse 1/Rhombergpassage, Telephone: 58 75 42

Glazing – Toy Manufacture – Picture Framing:
Paul Tollinger, Hofgasse 3, Telephone: 58 71 88, Fax: 57 82 23

Gläserkastl am Domplatz:
Domplatz,Telephone + Fax: 58 06 60

Blumenstüberl Floriana: Famous for its spice bouquets.
Hofgasse 2, Telephone: 58 39 58

Töpferstudio: High-quality ceramics artwork. Hans Jörg Kathrein, Viaduktbogen 1
Telephone: 57 32 18, Mondays – Fridays 8:30 am – 12:30 pm and 2 pm – 6 pm, Saturdays 8:30 am – 12 noon

Ceramics:
Lisa Waltl, Innstrasse 77,
Telephone: 29 10 41
The specialist shop for **pipe smokers:** Family-run shop for three generations produces traditional hand-crafted briar pipes. Lovingly hand-crafted pipes with modern design; customers have a voice in designing their own pipe. This is the secret to our success.
Karl Lorenz, Meinhardstrasse 13,
Telephone: 58 11 08

Tiroler Wachsindustrie: Manufacture of candles and wax products.
Carl Alois Walde, Pfarrgasse 5,
Telephone: 58 00 75

Candle Making: Traditional wax craftsmanship according to old peasant patterns.
Basilius Plank, Manufacture: Schneeburggasse 73,
Telephone: 28 33 26, Fax: 28 52 92.
Sales: Kunstklause, Seilergasse 9,
Telephone: 58 23 14

Metallkunst-Atelier: Manufacture and restoration of sacred objects; restoration of antique objects of gold, silver, brass, copper and tin; manufacture of funerary plaques and funerary objects; gold- and silver-plating.
Walter Deussl, St. Nikolausgasse 22, Telephone: 28 64 34

Master Shoemaker: Custom-made shoes (hand-sewn shoes, "hafele" shoes, hiking boots) and orthopedic shoes.
Adolf Staudinger, Leopoldstrasse 10,
Telephone: 58 44 05

Master Shoemaker: Walter Reithofer, Pradler Strasse 4,
Telephone: 48 5 19

Hat Maker: Albert Held, Burggraben 3, Telephone: 58 63 27, Mondays – Fridays 9 am – 6 pm, Saturdays 9 am – 12 noon.

Master Watchmaker: Workshop for antique clocks and watches; clocks and watches sold and purchased. Mario Loidold, Amraser Strasse 26,
Telephone: 36 43 16

Clocks – Jewelry – Antiques:
Georg Schmollgruber, Pfarrgasse 4,
Telephone: 58 84 22, Fax: 57 41 03

Gold-Plating – Mounting – Restoration:
Magda Lackner, Innstrasse 45,
Telephone: 29 51 17

Master Goldsmith:
Gabi Schneiderbauer, Domplatz 3,
Telephone: 58 91 56

Gold- and Silversmiths:
Traditional gold- and silversmith work since three generations. Austria's only filigree manufacturer. Many Tyrolean specialties: hand-made edelweiss (world famous), fortune rings, thimbles... Exclusive garnet jewelry in gold and silver!!!
Brigitte and Werner Bliem,
Herzog-Friedrich-Strasse 15 (Gol-

Silver filigree jewelry

den Roof), Telephone: 41 2 38 or 58 27 99

Horse Harnesses – Equestrian Sporting Goods – Quill Embroidery – Automobile Leather Goods: Günther Weiss, Langer Weg 26a, Telephone + Fax: 49 34 03

Lederhosen Manufacture: Custom-made solely of Austrian buckskin. Approx. 50 hours of work required per pair of breeches.
Walter Offner, Riedgasse 2, Telephone: 27 24 08

Leather Clothing and Quill Embroidery: Peter Nagele, Leopoldstrasse 35, Telephone: 58 01 25
World-famous **Swarovski** glassware sold at Herzog-Friedrich-Strasse 39, Telephone: 57 31 00

We also recommend a visit to **Tiroler Heimatwerk:** Meraner Strasse 2-4, Telephone: 58 23 20, where you can admire and purchase Tyrolean dress, typical Tyrolean souvenirs (mostly cottage industry), dinnerware of hand-painted pottery, wooden toys etc.

And in **Hall in Tirol:**
Turned Woodwork:
Leo Vonmetz, Agramgasse 23, Telephone: (05223) 56638
Glass Showcases – Glass Cutting:
Gerda Posch, Schlossergasse 13, Telephone: (05223) 42 9 60
Metalworking:
Helmut Brentel, Schlossergasse 13, Telephone: (05223) 57990
Metalworking:
Walter Graber, Schmiedgasse 20, Telephone: (05223) 56790
Master Blacksmith
Hermann Lamparter,Schmiedgasse 4, Telephone: (05223) 57366

SPORTS

Swimming

Freibad Tivoli (outdoor swimming pools): Purtschellerstrasse 1, Telephone: 34 23 44
Hallenbad (indoor pool) / Sauna: Amraser Str. 3, Phone: 34 25 85
Hallenbad (indoor pool) / Sauna Höttinger Au: Fürstenweg 12, Telephone: 28 23 39
Hallenbad (indoor pool) / Sauna Olympisches Dorf: Kugelfangweg 46, Telephone: 26 13 42
Dampfbad (Steambath) / Sauna: Salurner Straße 5, Telephone: 58 54 30
Baggersee – Rossau Recreation Area, open May – Sept, Telephone: 34 87 78

Ice-Skating

Eisstadion (Ice Stadium): Olympiastrasse 10
Telephone: 33 8 38

Skiing

Use the **Innsbruck Ski Pass** (good on all cable cars in Innsbruck, Igls, Mutters, Tulfes and Axamer Lizum) for free use of public transportation in Innsbruck and Igls and to Hungerburg. The Innsbruck Ski Pass also provides free admission to public indoor swimming pools. Obtainable at Innsbruck-Information (Burggraben 3), at the cable cars and funicular.

The ski resorts in Greater Innsbruck offer well-tended slopes for various degrees of skiing proficiency. For detailed information on ski courses, ski instructors etc., contact Innsbruck-Information (Burggraben 3) and the various cable cars (see p. 76). Free shuttle bus service to the ski resorts in Innsbruck, Igls, Tulfes, Mutters and Axams.

Cross-Country Skiing

The Club Innsbruck Card entitles you to free cross-country skiing instruction in Igls. Free shuttle buses take you to Tyrol's most beautiful cross-country tracks in Igls, Rinn, Natters, Gschnitztal, Gnadenwald, Pertisau, Seefeld and Leutasch.

Tobogganing

Well manicured toboggan runs are available in Heiligwasser, at Mutterer Alm, Birgitzer Alm, Kemater Alm and Rangger Köpfl.

Bobsleigh and Luge Run Igls

This run was built especially for the Olympic Winter Games. In the winter months it has since been the scene of numerous national and international bobsleigh, luge and skeleton competitions. For a breathtaking, unforgettable experience, take a ride in a guest bobsleigh. Reservations and information, Telephone: 37 75 25 or 37 71 60

Mountain Hiking Program

Mountain hikes are conducted in the summer months, organized by Alpinschule Innsbruck. Participation is free for holders of the Club Innsbruck Card. For information, contact Innsbruck-Igls Tourist Office, Burggraben 3, Innsbruck-Information, Burggraben 3, or Alpinschule Innsbruck, Hannes Gasser, In der Stille 1, A-6161 Natters, Telephone: 54 60 00, Fax: 54 60 01.

Rock Climbing

The **Innsbruck Panorama-Klettersteig** (fixed-rope climbing route) leads from Hafelekar (Nordkette) over seven peaks to Frau-Hitt-Sattel. It can be climbed in approx. 4 1/2 hrs. but only in summer. The **climbing trail (Klettersteig) on Martinswand** should only be attempted by experienced alpinists, because its lower portion to the Maximilian Grotto (1 hr.) is rated very difficult and its upper portion (1 1/2 hrs.) extremely difficult. Due to its southern exposure, it can be climbed almost all year 'round.

Before starting out on a climbing trail, be certain you are surefooted, do not get dizzy and are outfitted with special climbing equipment.

Klettergarten in the old Hötting stone quarry
Alpenverein-Klettergarten Martinswand

The challenging climbing trail on Martinswand

For further information, contact the **Austrian Alpine Club:** Wilhelm-Greil-Strasse 15, Telephone: 59 5 47

Fitness Trails

Amras: Starts near main entrance to Ambras Castle
Kranebitten: Starts near camp-grounds

Indoor Tennis and Squash

Tennis and Squash Center: Stadlweg 40, Telephone: 34 44 14
Tennishalle allround: Wiesengasse 16, Telephone: 36 01 10
Tennishalle ARGE: Falkstrasse 4, Telephone: 57 18 39
Tennishalle Neu-Rum: Steinbockallee 28, Telephone: 26 34 20
Tennishallen West: Fürstenweg 172, Telephone: 28 43 64
Tennisclub IEV: Reichenauer Strasse 144, Telephone: 34 62 29
Tennishalle/Parkclub Igls: Kurpark, Telephone: 37 76 38

Horseback Riding

Campagnereiter-Gesellschaft/Tirol: Langer Weg 43, Telephone: 34 71 74

Official Mountainbike Trails

From Sadrach via Höttinger Bild to Achselkopf.
From Hungerburg via Arzler Alm to Höttinger Alm and on to Bodensteinalm.
From Mühlau through Mühlauer Klamm (gorge) to Arzler Alm and from there to Höttinger Alm and Bodensteinalm.
From Patsch via Patscher Alm to Patscherkofelhaus and on to the peak.

If you require **information** on other sports or sporting goods rental agencies, please contact Innsbruck-Information.

Or would you rather be a specta-tor at a major sports event?

An annual highpoint on Innsbruck's sports calendar is the Intersport Ski Jumping Tourna-ment at Bergisel. This is the ski jump where the ski jumping events for the 1964 and 1976 Olympic Winter Games were held. In the winter months the Olympic Bobsleigh and Luge Run in Igls is the scene of various national and international competitions.

POST OFFICE AND TELEPHONE SERVICE

Post- und Telegrafendirektion für Tirol und Vorarlberg: Maximilianstrasse 2, Telephone: 500, Fax: 55 27 80

Main Post Office
Maximilianstrasse 2, 6010 Innsbruck, open Mondays – Sundays 24 hours a day, Telephone: 500

Railroad Post Office
Brunecker Strasse 1– 3, 6020 Innsbruck, open Mondays – Saturdays 6:30 am – 9 pm, Telephone: 59 9 34

Additional Post Offices:
Open Mondays – Fridays 8 am – 12 noon and 2 pm – 6 pm, some post offices open Saturdays 8 am – 12 noon
Stainerstrasse 3, 6012 Innsbruck, Telephone: 58 28 11
Franz-Fischer-Strasse 5, 6013 Innsbruck, Telephone: 58 28 47
Claudiastrasse 12, 6014 Innsbruck, Telephone: 58 13 01
Prinz-Eugen-Strasse 60, 6022 Innsbruck, Telephone: 35 12 30
Gumppstrasse 26, 6023 Innsbruck, Telephone: 35 12 00
Schulgasse 3, 6024 Innsbruck, Telephone: 27 11 70
Anton-Rauch-Strasse 39, 6025 Innsbruck, Telephone: 26 18 10
Fischnalerstrasse 4, 6026 Innsbruck, Telephone: 27 11 51
Viktor-Franz-Hess-Strasse, 6027 Innsbruck, Telephone: 27 11 60
Amraser-See-Strasse 56a, 6029 Innsbruck, Telephone: 35 12 52
Schnellmanngasse 2, 6033 Innsbruck, Telephone: 26 18 01
Schützenstrasse 54, 6040 Innsbruck, Telephone: 26 18 50
Igls, 6080 Igls, Telephone: 37 70 30

Telephone Information:
Telephone: 08
Telegram Office (outgoing):
Telephone: 190
Area codes from Innsbruck to

Germany	0049
Italy	0039
Switzerland	0041
France	0033
United States	001
United Kingdom	0044

CONSULATES AND EMBASSIES

Belgium: Erlerstrasse 9, Telephone: 53 33
Denmark: Maria-Theresien-Strasse 42, Telephone: 58 29 71
Finland: Bozner Platz 6, Telephone: 58 38 63
France: Maria-Theresien-Strasse 24, Telephone: 58 47 93
Germany: Adamgasse 5, Telephone: 59 6 65
Hungary: Haller Strasse 15, Telephone: 26 69 44
Italy: Conradstrasse 9, Telephone: 58 13 33 or 58 49 83
Netherlands: Salurner Strasse 15, Telephone: 58 74 92
Norway: Erlerstrasse 9, Telephone: 53 33
Sweden: Andreas-Hofer-Strasse 43, Telephone: 57 18 71
Switzerland: Höhenstrasse 107, Telephone: 29 22 21
United Kingdom: Matthias-Schmid-Strasse 12
Telephone: 58 83 20

Hall with the Bettelwurf ▸

HALL IN TIROL

Autonomous, yet almost touching fingertips with Innsbruck is the city of Hall in Tirol. The old salt and coinage city is a jewel of medieval urban planning with narrow stairways and back alleys, battlements embellished with coats of arms, lovely oriels, Gothic frescoes and beautiful churches. In the well-preserved city wall is the fortified Hasegg Castle with the Mint Gate (Münzertor) and Mint Tower (Münzerturm), where today's visitors can strike commemorative coins themselves.

Hall in Tirol, about 10 km east of Innsbruck on the left bank of the Inn, has a population of approx. 12,500. The name "Halle" means a "place to boil salt" and was first officially documented in 1263. In the nearby Hall Valley (Halltal) salt mining played an important role, even in prehistoric times. The salt was transported on the Roman road from Hall via Igls and Ellbögen to Brenner Pass and on to Italy, where it was traded for tropical fruits and wine.

CHRONICLE OF HALL IN TIROL

1232/1256
New **settlements** spring up near the **salt works,** for example Thaur and Hall. Great economic boom due to the extraction and processing of salt as well as shipping activity on the Inn.

1286
Hall rises to the status of a **market town.**

1303
Duke Otto grants Hall its **city charter,** meaning the same rights and privileges already held by Innsbruck. Hall becomes a prosperous community. The fortified Old City with its walls and towers is twice as large as Innsbruck's.

1356
Hall acquires the right to hold **markets** for eight days twice a year. Up to the 18th century, these remain the most important markets throughout the region.

1420
Duke Frederick moves his **residence** from Meran to **Innsbruck.** Hall increasingly declines in importance.

1477
Duke Sigismund "the Rich" transfers the **mint** from Meran to the old **Sparberegg Castle** in Hall. The "Haller Thaler" minted in 1486 was the world's first large silver coin.

1534 – 1630
Archduke Ferdinand II founds the royal **glassworks** in Scheibenegg.

Double-sided gulden of Emperor Maximilian I from 1508, designed by Ulrich Ursentaler and minted in Hall

1567
Archduke Ferdinand II transfers the **mint** to **Hasegg Castle.** The Mint Tower (Münzerturm), the city's landmark, is a lasting reminder.

1570
Archduke Ferdinand II's sisters, Magdalena, Helene and Margarethe, found the **Hall Noblewomen's Convent (Haller Damenstift),** which is to have great cultural and economic influence on the city and is an important commissioner of artists and craftsmen. In 1783 the institution is dissolved.

15th – 18th century
On the Inn is the **"Lende,"** berth and stock terminal for all grain imports from the east to Tyrol. The log-catching device on the Inn, which intercepts logs from the Upper Inn Valley and even the Engadine that are vital to the extraction of salt, prevents ships from continuing upriver. Hall thus becomes an important river port.

18th century
The **importance of salt mining** and **shipping** on the Inn **begins to wane.**

1858/1867
Railroad construction to the Lower Inn Valley and over Brenner Pass gives Innsbruck priority over Hall for commercial traffic.

1938
Heiligkreuz is incorporated into the city. The city is renamed **"Solbad Hall."**

1967
Due to a lack of profitability, the **salt mines are closed.**

1975
The **Old Mint is restored** in Hasegg Castle. This is where the coins commemorating the 1976 Winter Olympic Games in Innsbruck were minted.

Since 1975
Numerous buildings in the **Old City** have been and continue to undergo costly **restoration** and **revitalization;** old cultural treasures remain while new apartments and commercial premises are created. Precious paintings and frescoes inside and outside the buildings have been brought to light and restored, including the following: Wallpachgasse 4 (Gothic vines winding around a door), Wallpachgasse 6 (Gothic jousting fresco), Mustergasse 2 (view of Hall c. 1500 and Gothic frescoes from the former façade c. 1500).

View to the Sacred Heart Basilika

CITY SIGHTS

Allerheiligenkirche (Church of All Saints)

The former Jesuit church, an Early Baroque hall, was constructed in 1608 by the Jesuit Stefan Huber. Note the Baroque main altar with a painting of the saints by Mathias Kager from 1609, the statues of St. Peter and St. Paul on the sides and the priceless tabernacle of ebony with silverwork and Baroque stuccowork. Because of its unique acoustics, many church concerts are given here. In the northwest of the nave is the Chapel of St. Francis Xavier, added in 1663. The former Jesuit Monastery adjoins the building in the north and now houses the county court. It contains one of Tyrol's loveliest Baroque courtyards.

★ Burg Hasegg (Hasegg Castle)

Duke Sigismund converted the old Sparberegg Castle, located at the southeast corner of the city and first documented in 1263, to the mint in 1477. He simultaneously began systematic expansion of the southern part of the salt works, which was referred to as "Pfannhaus-Eck," whence the name "Hausegg" and later "Hasegg." In 1489 construction of the castle was completed. The castle protected shipping operations and river crossings. Further expansion followed at the beginning of the 16th century under Emperor Maximilian I.

Archduke Ferdinand II transferred

The landmark Mint Tower in Hall in Tirol

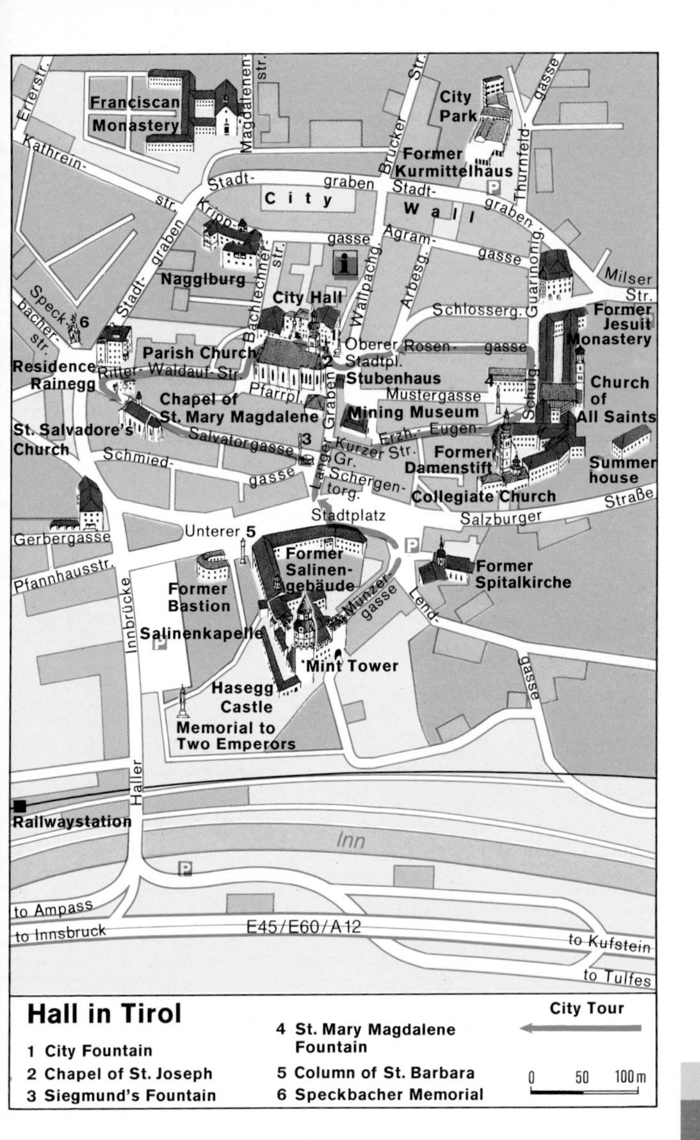

the mint to the castle in 1567. In 1809 there was a temporary end to coin minting in Hasegg Castle and the castle fell into ruin. Between 1974 and 1977 costly and intensive restoration efforts were begun and the castle was revitalized as a cultural center. It now houses the Municipal Museum, the Old Mint etc. You can even mint a commemorative coin here! The Galerie St. Barbara hosts exhibits, while concerts and plays are presented in the picturesque Gothic courtyard. The inn in the castle invites you to a well-deserved rest and refreshment.

The castle is an erratic structure built around a central courtyard. In the southwest corner is the Mint Tower, Hall's landmark building. It contains the so-called Princes' Hall (Fürstensaal) with a splendid Late Gothic timber ceiling.

The Chapel of St. George on the first floor of the east tract was constructed between 1515 and 1519 according to plans by Niclas Türing the Elder and his son Gregor. Of particular interest in this chapel with its net vaults are the Baroque altar with a statue of St. George flanked by St. Sebastian and St. Florian and the paintings.

Franziskanerkirche und -kloster (Franciscan Church and Monastery)

This complex is located in the northwest part of the city, outside the Stadtgraben (city moat), and was built in the mid 17th century. The interior decor of the church underwent thorough renovation in 1880. Franz Hellweger's high altar painting of the Virgin Mary and the four angels also dates back to this time. Also note the left side altar with the Baroque painting of the Virgin Mary and the right side altar with a relief of St. Francis and angels playing music by resident artist Josef Bachlechner Sr. (1917). Paintings by Christoph Anton Mayr (1760) depicting the life and deeds of St. Francis hang in the cross-vaulted cloister. The adjoining monastery building, a simple, two-story structure has undergone many changes and much expansion since the 17th century. Since the 18th century, the Franciscan monks have run a boarding school for high school students, the "Leopoldinum," which is well-known throughout Tyrol.

Herz-Jesu-Basilika, ehemalige Damenstift und Stiftskirche (Sacred Heart Basilica, Former Damenstift and Collegiate Church)

This structure was erected on the site of the former Sparberegg Castle (Old Mint). The Collegiate Church, a baroqued Renaissance building, was constructed from 1567 to 1570, reportedly by Giovanni Luchese. The earthquake of 1670 caused severe damage to the church, which necessitated its renovation and redecoration in the Baroque style. After the Noblewomen's Convent (Damenstift) was dissolved in 1783, many of its furnishings were destroyed and the church was secularized until 1786. In 1912, the church was reconsecrated; the decor dates from this period. On the north side of the church is the tomb and a portrait of Archduchess Magdalena, one of the founders of the Damenstift.

After the convent was secularized, a hospital was installed in the building. Since 1912, nuns have reinhabited the building. The convent has a noteworthy Renaissance cloister. The Damenstift's former summer house decorated with exquisite wall and ceiling paintings by Kaspar Waldmann (1716) is located in the former convent garden and dates back to 1715. It is now privately owned.

Magdalenen-Kapelle (Chapel of St. Mary Magdalene)

In earlier times the cemetery and various chapels surrounded the Parish Church of St. Nicholas. The chapel dedicated to Saint Mary Magdalene possesses a priceless Late Gothic carved altarpiece and beautiful frescoes dating back to 1410.

★ Rathaus (City Hall)

On the west end of Oberer Stadtplatz lies the three-story City Hall building, which served as the city residence of Tyrol's rulers until the Counts of Tyrol died out in 1363. Duke Leopold IV made a gift of it to the city in 1406, and it has hence served as City Hall. The Late Gothic timbered ceiling, the wall panelling and the doors with beautiful woodwork in the building's main hall are especially worth seeing.

★ Stadtpfarrkirche zum hl. Nikolaus (Parish Church of St. Nicholas)

The church was first consecrated in 1281. St. Nicholas is the patron saint of miners and sailors. Reconstruction of the choir was begun in the early 14th century, while the Gothic tower was completed in 1345 and the single-span Gothic nave in 1352. Between 1420 and 1437, Hans Sewer expanded the nave to the north and west and converted it to a three-span structure. The church's location produces an interesting effect by forcing the nave into an asymmetric relation with the choir. The Fieger Chapel, the tomb of an influential Hall family, was added in the 15th century; the tower was done over at the same time and then baroqued in the 16th century. The interior of the church was done in the Baroque style in 1752 by Josef Adam Mölk. He also created the ceiling frescoes, which depict scenes from St. Nicholas' life. Only a precious few remnants of the Gothic glass windows survive. On the northern wall of the church's nave are faded bits of Gothic frescoes. The two large Renaissance epitaphs of painted wood in the choir are not to be overlooked. A painting of the "Madonna with Saints" by Erasmus Quellinus, a student of Rubens, adorns the high altar (1657). The statues of the apostles and church fathers on the walls of the choir, just as the side altar, date back to the 18th century. Martin Altomonte painted the Mater Dolorosa on the north wall in 1740. The year 1506 is inscribed on the holy water font of red marble.

Christ on Palm Donkey

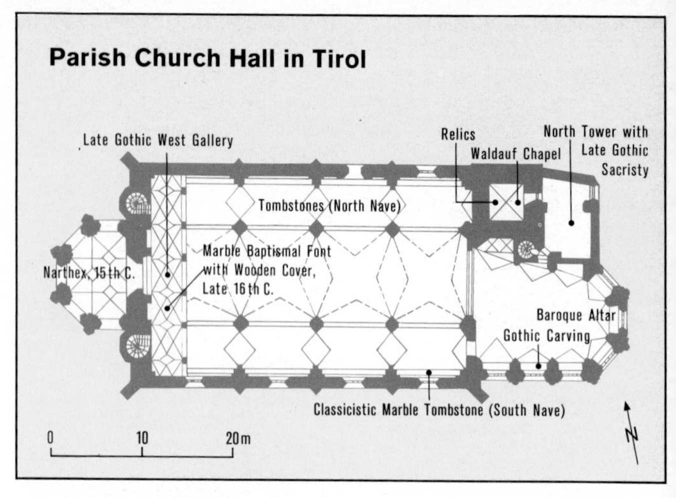

Make note of the Gothic woodcarving in the choir depicting "Christ on Palm Donkey," which is used in the Palm Sunday procession.

In 1495 Sir Florian Waldauf and his wife donated the Waldauf Chapel, which bears their name, in the east bay of the church's side aisle. The Waldauf Chapel is separated from the rest of the church by an elaborate Gothic grille. Be sure to note the Baroque altar, by Christoph Wörndle, with a Late Gothic carved statue of the Madonna (reputedly by Michael Pacher), and the glass cases on the north wall holding the remnants of the Waldauf collection of relics (religious treasure of Hall).

MUSEUMS

Bergbaumuseum (Mining Museum)

Oberer Stadtplatz 1
Telephone: (0 52 23) 56 2 69 or 58 45
Open: guided tours only. Apr – Oct Mondays – Saturdays on the hour 9 am – 11 am and 2 pm – 5 pm
The museum is dedicated to salt mining, which was of such importance to Hall for centuries. Mining is illustrated here in life-size tunnels, shafts, chutes etc.; various minerals are also on display. The Salt Mining Museum in the "Herrenhaus" in Hall Valley (Absam) is an affiliate.

Stadtmuseum in der Burg Hasegg (Municipal Museum in Hasegg Castle)

Unterer Stadtplatz
Telephone: (0 52 23) 52 4 11
Open: guided tours only. Apr – Oct Mondays – Saturdays on the hour 10 am, 11 am, 2 pm – 5 pm Sundays and public holidays on the hour 2 pm – 5 pm, or by prior arrangement by telephone.

Highlights: history of the city, guilds, coins, salt works and religious art

Alte Münze in der Burg Hasegg (Old Mint in Hasegg Castle)

Burg Hasegg 6
Telephone: (0 52 23) 44 2 45
or 41 31
Open: Mondays – Thursdays 8 am – 12 noon and 2 pm – 6 pm; Fridays 8 am – 12 noon, or by prior arrangement by telephone.
Highlight: coin minting

INFORMATION

Information
Hall in Tirol Tourist Office
Wallpachgasse 5
A-6060 Hall in Tirol
Telephone: (0 52 23) 56 2 69
or 56 2 20
Fax: (0 52 23) 56 2 20 20
Open: Mondays – Fridays 9 am – 12 noon and 2 pm – 6 pm; Saturdays 9 am – 12 noon

City Tours of Hall in Tirol
Apr – Oct Mondays – Saturdays
10 am and 2 pm
Reservations with the Hall in Tirol Tourist Office are recommended. Rendezvous at the Tourist Office; on Saturdays only, rendezvous at Hasegg Castle.

Campgrounds
Scheidensteinstrasse 24 (next to the outdoor pool)
Telephone: (0 52 23) 45 4 64
open May – Sept

Bus Service to Innsbruck
Bus line 4 via the city streets
Bus line S via the autobahn

Pay Car Parks (indoors)
West of the Parkhotel

Krankenhaus Hall (Hall District Hospital)
Milser Strasse 10
Telephone: (0 52 23) 502

Landes-Nervenkrankenhaus (State Psychiatric Hospital)
Thurnfeldgasse 14
Telephone: (0 52 23) 58 91

Post Offices
Essacherstrasse 15-17
A-6050 Hall in Tirol
Telephone: (0 52 23) 58 09

Krippgasse 7-9
A-6060 Hall in Tirol
Telephone: (0 52 23) 58 08

Coat of arms of Jörg Fueger on City Hall (1387)

INDEX

Items marked with * are found in Hall in Tirol.

Adolf-Pichler-Platz 50
Alpine Club Museum 55
Alpine Zoo 61
Ambras Castle..............................35
Andreas-Hofer-Strasse..................50
Anichstrasse 50
Arch of Triumph............................43
Art Room, Servite Monastery 57
Basilica of Wilten 14
Bell Museum..................................55
Bergisel 17
Bergisel (Kaiserjäger) Museum....55
Blasius-Hueber-Strasse................50
Bobsleigh and Luge Run Igls 84
Botanical Garden..........................62
Büchsenhausen............................17
Butterfly House 62
Cathedral of St. James 18
Chapel of St. Mary Magdalene....93*
Church of All Saints.....................90*
Church of Our Lady of Perpetual Help 33
Church of St. Nicholas..................34
Church of St. Nicholas 93*
City Hall..93*
City Tower 13
Colingasse.....................................50
Column of St. Anne 14
Congress Center 31
Court Church 25
Court Garden................................25
Court Palace.................................23
Cranachstrasse 50
Domplatz 21
Erzherzog-Eugen-Strasse 50
Europe Bridge.........................67/68
Fennerstrasse...............................50
Franciscan Church and Monastery...............................92*
Fugger-Taxis Palace 34
Gilmstrasse...................................50
Golden Roof 21
Grassmayrstrasse 51
Gumpp Family 44
Gumppstrasse 44
Hasegg Castle............................90*
Haspingerstrasse.........................51
Haymongasse...............................51
Heiligwasser - Pilgrimage Church 22
Helblinghaus.................................51
Herzog-Friedrich-Strasse 51
Herzog-Otto-Strasse.....................52
Herzog-Sigmund-Ufer...................52
Hospital Church 38
Hungerburg...................................63
Hungerburg - Church of St. Theresa 30
Igls - Church of St. Giles...............30
Imperial Rifle Regiment Museum .56
Innsbruck Panorama-Klettersteig .84
Jesuit Church................................30
Kaiserjägerstrasse........................52
Karl-Rahner-Platz.........................52
Karl-Schönherr-Strasse................52
Köldererstrasse 52
Leopold Fountain..........................31
Maria-Theresien-Strasse..............53
Maximilianstrasse.........................53
Meinhardstrasse...........................53
Mining Museum...........................94*
Municipal Archive 58
Municipal Museum, Hasegg Castle..........................94*
Museum of Fine Art 56
Museum of Tyrolean Folk Art 59
Natural Sciences Collection 57
New City Hall 33
New Monastery 27
Old City Hall..................................13
Olympic Museum..........................57
Ottoburg 34
Panorama Painting of Bergisel.....58
Patscherkofel................................66
Philippine-Welser-Strasse 53
Premonstratensian Abbey Museum 58
Regional Train Museum 57
Rennweg 53
Rudolf Fountain 34
Sacred Heart Basilica, former Damenstift and Collegiate Church....................................92*
Salt Mining Museum 94*
Servite Church..............................38
Silver Chapel 27
Ski Jump.......................................39
Speckbacherstrasse.....................53
State Capital Building 33
Traklpark 54
Tyrolean Regional Museum - Armory 59
Tyrolean State Museum Ferdinandeum......................42/58
Tyrolean State Theater.................31
University......................................43
Wilten Abbey Church and Premonstratensian Abbey in Wilten 40